In this scholarly book an eminent Continental theologian examines the basis and the nature of the Christian faith, finding it to consist in man's freedom from the world and his freedom for God.

Christ's redemptive action demonstrated the nothingness of the world, proclaimed man as God's son and the inheritor of the world, and established the true focal point of man's life, namely, the Creator God.

That man should be God-centered and not world-centered was the basis of Paul's doctrine of justification by faith, and a considerable part of the present volume is devoted to a penetrating exegesis of the Pauline theology. Man had to be freed from bondage to ritualism and legalism so that, as God's child, he could walk in the liberty whereinto he had been called.

This doctrine of freedom was further developed in Reformation times by Martin Luther. It is not a man's actions, even good actions, that God requires of him; it is the man himself. " Man should be good. But he will not become good through works. The works will be good through him."

The throwing off of the trammels of priestly authority in the secular world released modern man to another kind of freedom — unlimited scientific experimentation. This freedom is in itself good, but it is beset by a danger similar to that against which Paul and Luther inveighed, the danger of worshiping the creature instead of the Cre-

THE REALITY OF FAITH

THE REALITY OF FAITH

The Problem of Subjectivism in Theology

by FRIEDRICH GOGARTEN

Translated by Carl Michalson and Others

THE WESTMINSTER PRESS • Philadelphia

Translation of *Die Wirklichkeit des Glaubens,* Zum Problem des Subjektivismus in der Theologie. Friedrich Vorwerk Verlag, Stuttgart, Germany, 1957.

Library of Congress Catalog Card No. 59–5048

PRINTED IN THE UNITED STATES OF AMERICA

CONTENTS

TRANSLATOR'S PREFACE

This book has been brought into English under circumstances involving a great many people. First of all, President Fred G. Holloway and Dean Stanley R. Hopper, of Drew University, had the vision to invite Professor Gogarten as Visiting Professor of Biblical Theology in the Graduate School during the academic year 1957–1958. This book, which was just about to appear in Germany, was chosen as the basis for his first course of lectures.

Immediately Ted Runyan, a Drew graduate completing his doctorate at the University of Göttingen, translated the first three chapters and set up a lexicon of the more specialized words. With this as a basis, a whole group of Drew graduates and graduate students who had either studied in Germany or achieved a measure of competence in the German language assisted me in translating the remainder of the volume. Marjorie Chambers and Richard Underwood each completed more than a chapter. The other contributors were Prof. Robert Osborn, of Duke University, James Dickinson, Ira Zepp, Karl Wright, and Garnett Wilder. Pat Winters typed the manuscript.

A valuable aid in the preparation of this volume was a complete English version created by Professor Gogarten himself primarily as an exercise in the language. Professor Runyan, now of the Candler School of Theology, Emory University, was in constant dialogue with Professor Gogarten during that process, just as I have been in completing the translation and attempting to bring the whole volume into linguistic unity.

I speak for this entire group when I say how pleased we are to be associated with The Westminster Press in giving American readers their first full-scale reading of Professor Gogarten's theology. Any infelicities in this handling of his profound and exacting insights should be charged to me alone.

One should be warned, however, that Professor Gogarten conceives his theology almost symphonically. A great variety of themes are introduced throughout, sometimes vaguely, recurring and blending together more convincingly as the discussion unfolds. His literary strategy emulates the detective story. The important clues are withheld, to be revealed only where they will illuminate the plot most effectively. Like a genuinely creative novelist, he need not know at the beginning of his story what he knows at the end. Why, therefore, should the reader expect to? It is to be hoped, therefore, that the reader will not impatiently abandon as bad translation what is, rather, a sophisticated and rigorously developed theological method.

CARL MICHALSON

Drew Forest
Madison, N.J.

1. THE SUPERNATURAL UNDERSTANDING OF FAITH

The theme I shall be dealing with in this volume is " the reality of the Christian faith," with special reference to the problem of subjectivism in theology. Subjectivism as well as faith is the reality that concerns theology. It is a unique kind of reality in the respect that it is a reality that is believed in. What does this mean? First of all, of course, it means that it is not a sensual reality, a reality one can see with the eyes or touch or grasp with the hands. For, according to The Letter to the Hebrews, faith is " the assurance of things hoped for, the conviction of things not seen " (Heb. 11:1). What Paul says to the Romans concerning hope is just as applicable to faith. " Hope that is seen is not hope." (Rom. 8:24.) A reality that can be seen with the eyes and grasped with the hands can be proved to be " really there," even if for one reason or another we no longer see it. But a reality in which one hopes or believes cannot be demonstrated. In other words, one cannot prove it is really there if " really " refers not only to what is believed but also to what is outside of and independent of faith. But the reality that concerns theology is faith in God. If the God in whom faith believes were not real outside of faith and independent of it, this faith would lose all sense. What kind of reality is it, then? This is the question before us here. How is this reality experienced, how can man become aware of it, how can he perceive it? How is it related to the reality that can be seen and grasped, the reality that is immediately demonstrated in its being seen and grasped?

Clearly this is one of theology's most important questions, if not the most important. For the discipline of theology is intent upon giving an " account " of the reality of faith. Its purpose is to say what one believes in, to say in what sense what one believes in is real and not just imagined or produced by speculation, and to say how it stands in relation to the reality approachable immediately or by reason of cogent conclusions derived from the immediately given. This book will not concern itself, however, with a historical presentation of the way the question of the reality of faith has been asked and answered in the course of the history of theology. The account theology gives of the reality of faith cannot remain the same down through the ages, simply because the question of reality has been asked and answered at different times in such different ways. Such an account is meaningful and can be communicated only when it is pursued, not just with a view to the particular reality that concerns theology, but in dialogue with the general understanding of reality prevailing at any given time. But this book will not detail the historical development of the forms of such theological bookkeeping. Instead, we shall try to deal with the question of the reality of faith as it is raised in our own time by the understanding of reality that is current.

Nevertheless, to gain an initial orientation to the context in which this question is posed for us today, we would do well to take a cursory glance at how the question has been asked and answered prior to our time. On the one hand, such a review can help us to recognize what we should be asking. On the other hand, it can help us to achieve the freedom necessary for asking our own questions, the questions evoked by our time. For it is all too easy to get bogged down in formulations and conceptions composed in a situation entirely different from the one we face. The kind of reality that theology asks about is the reality of God and his revelation. Because this is an eternal, unchanging reality, it is not difficult to understand why theological questions and answers, along with the concepts used to formulate them, tend to preserve their validity beyond the time in which they were truly valid. But this could easily make us unaware of those questions which meet us out of our own understanding of reality in the present. Consequently, the answers given would not be understood and therefore could not be compelling. For this initial orientation to the context in which the question of the reality of faith is asked, I wish to choose the theology of the Middle Ages. Therefore, in this first chapter I shall deal with the supernatural understanding of the reality of the Christian faith.

The reason for choosing medieval theology is that its whole scheme determines our theological thinking more than we are usually aware. Now, when we turn from our own time and its problems to the world of the Middle Ages, what will doubtless seem the strangest to us there is the sense of a pre-established order influencing the whole of life and its contents, an order that was eternally given for all time. This does not necessarily mean that the order was everywhere and always observed, or that it always took the same form during the whole medieval era. It means, rather, that the order then in force had a static character and was therefore regarded as valid for all times and circumstances. In contrast to this, the modern man finds it natural to assume that the orders of his world can have only a historical validity. For him, they are subordinate to the historical movements of the world in which he lives and in which he finds his reality. He is thoroughly aware of the fact that these orders have been discovered by men in the process of history and that they must be ever discovered anew in responsibility for the life that has to be lived in them. When I said that the order of the medieval world was a pre-established order, I meant that this order, in contrast to the orders of the modern world, was understood not as something developed in the history of man for which man was therefore responsible, but rather as something that is and always has been valid as long as the world has been and will be. In this eternally existing order, the world has its reality.

In the context of this concept of reality, medieval theology gave its account of the reality of God and his revelation. It did so by understanding it as the reality from which the world proceeded and to which the world is therefore subordinate. The reality of God is a supernatural reality. The reality of the world, however, is a natural reality. The implications of these two kinds of reality become clear in the concept of " law." The eternal law (*lex aeterna*) corresponds to the reality of God. The natural law (*lex naturalis*) corresponds to the reality of the world. According to Thomas Aquinas, " law " in this context means " a rational ordering for the common good proclaimed by the one who cares for the community " (*rationis ordinatio ad bonum commune, ab eo, qui curam communitatis habet, promulgata*). The relation of the eternal and the natural law to each other is explained in this way: the natural law is the participation of the eternal law in the rational creature, that is, in the human reason (*lex naturalis nihil aliud est quam participatio legis aeternae in rationali creatura*). Because that is so, it follows that the natural law should be regarded as the same for all peoples everywhere and in all times.

To understand the phenomenon of natural law through the concept of participation is utterly decisive. For through it a continuity can be conceived between two realities, the reality of God and the reality of the world. Everything creaturely exists within that continuity. To be sure, the continuity has been weakened by the Fall of man. But it has not been destroyed. Man lost the supernatural grace

God had bestowed on him in Paradise. That grace, which was a perfection in which man was able to see God as God sees himself, transcended man's purely creaturely nature. It is called the *donum superadditum,* the superadded gift. God added this perfection to man's essential humanity. It must be distinguished from man's natural or creaturely perfection. When it was lost by the Fall, man nevertheless retained everything that constitutes his nature in its creaturely being, including even the powers of the soul and similar powers. To be sure, the inclination to do what the natural law demands (*inclinatio ad debitum actum et finem*) , though not fully destroyed, has been severely weakened. The good demanded by the natural law is the natural good (*bonum naturae*) , the good that corresponds to God's creation.

I would venture to say that this is mainly the scheme within which medieval theology sought to lay hold of the reality of the divine revelation and its relation to the reality of the world man lives in. The divine reality as understood by the theology of the Middle Ages was of course the church, the church as *corpus Christi mysticum,* the mystical body of Christ. As the body of Christ, who is the God-man in whom both nature and supernature are united, the church embraces all of reality within itself. It embraces the reality of God as well as the reality of the world, the supernatural reality as well as the natural reality. It is the purpose of the church in this understanding not just to check any deepening of the flaw that the Fall insinuated into the continuity between the reality of God and the world. It is the purpose of the church to restore the two again to their original continuity. The church is able to do this only because it is regarded by this theology as the hierarchical order of all being. The hierarchical order of being puts everything in its proper relation, from the most spiritual being of God to the most material qualities of man's worldly life. Moreover, this is not just a relation in thought. It is a relation of the greatest effectual power, intimately reuniting these two realities.

The mystery of the unification of God with man and his world has its deepest manifestation in the incarnation of God in the man Jesus Christ. The seven sacraments derive their power from this incarnation. By means of these sacraments, the church embraces the whole life of man, reuniting his life in all its heights and depths with the reality of God, and thereby sanctifying it. From the incarnation also come the many blessings and consecrations with which the church through its priests brings everything into the presence of the divine reality, from the most exalted orders of human life, such as the crowning of emperors and kings in the Middle Ages, to the most ordinary things. Each is brought before God in the manner appropriate to its nature. As Hans Freyer writes in *Weltgeschichte Europas* (p. 689): "Thus in every hour the wonder of transubstantiation is consummated. The hand that grasps the sword, the plow, and the chisel at the same time reaches into the other world and takes a piece of salvation. Monks work and fight, though their special task in the world is to pray; knights and kings pray, though their office in the world is to rule: never . . . has the Kingdom of God come so near the earth as here; never did everything earthly become so completely symbolic."

One comment still has to be made regarding the method and manner in which the sacraments of the church operate. Their effect should be viewed in an entirely realistic way. "The church does not attenuate the sacrament into an empty symbol, or into a sign of grace which obtains all its efficacy from subjective faith. On the contrary, it is a real expression of our Lord's gracious will, a sign of Christ (*signum Christi*), and as such it already ensures the presence of his grace through itself, through its actual performance." In this context it is valid to say that "a sacrament is not fulfilled by the fact that one believes in it, but by the fact that it is performed." They effect what they signify. (*Sacramenta efficiunt quod figurant.*) Hence, in the sacraments the divine grace assumes " tangible reality." It is visibly present. (Karl Adam, *The Spirit of Catholicism,* p. 197; Image Books.) The statement to the effect that " a sacrament is fulfilled not by the fact that one believes in it, but by the fact that it is performed " obviously ought not to be understood to mean that faith should be excluded. As Karl Adam says, " When it is a question of the sanctification of an adult who has attained religious and moral consciousness, the recipient must prepare himself subjectively for the grace which is objectively imparted in the sacramental act, by acts of faith, contrition, and repentance." These subjective acts by the recipient of the sacraments, however, are " not the effective cause of his sanctification, its *causa efficiens,* but only its preparatory cause, *causa dispositiva* " (*ibid.,* pp. 24-25). The way this preparatory cause is to be understood becomes clear when we see that faith as the preparatory cause is necessary for the valid appropriation of the sacramental grace. But the preparation can already be attained, although only in the slightest degree, if one does not set in opposition to the sacrament a mentality that is hostile to it (*obex contrariae cogitationis*), denying it as such.

Although what I have said has been brief, I hope it has helped to clarify the concept of reality with which medieval theology sought to lay hold of the reality of God's revelation. I hope it has also clarified the nature of the correlation by which theology, using this concept, united the reality of God with the reality of the world. The concept I refer to is the idea of metaphysical reality as originally formulated by Greek philosophy and later used by theology to account for what is believed by the Christian faith. As I have indicated, such an account can be meaningful and compelling only when it occurs in dialogue with the reality of the world as generally understood in any given era. According to Wilhelm Dilthey, one can characterize the actual condition of the medieval man's world in this way: " The life of state was retrogressing from the Roman form to a natural form; individuals remained in the primitive natural relation to the soil; universal precepts of law were giving way to individualistic human elements in personal relations and tribal bonds. Added to these factors was the youthful impetuousness of the Teutonic race which was pumping new blood into the older races. All these factors added together resulted in a boundless life of the senses and the will." At the same time, Dilthey continues, " in the soul of medieval man, faith in a transcendental realm battled against these forces. The weapons of this transcendental realm were church, priest, and sacrament. Through these it worked its influence on this world, continuously radiating its divine powers" (*Einleitung in die Geisteswissenschaften,* p. 353). When medieval man sought to achieve intellectual and conceptual clarity regarding the wholeness of his world, the only instrument at his disposal was Greek philosophy, in so far as he was acquainted with it. With the metaphysical concepts of Greek philosophy, medieval theology conceived the reality of God as well as the reality of man's world in terms of a metaphysical realm. This realm was governed by a hierarchical order of being, with God the Creator as the eternal Head. As Dilthey says, it was an order stretching " from the throne of God down to the last peasant's hut, creating an immense reality comprehensible to the man of the Middle Ages. This reality is at the base of all speculations about history and society in medieval metaphysics." (*Ibid.,* p. 329.)

As I said at the outset, to gain an orientation to the context that raises the question of the reality of God and his revelation today, we would do well to recall how this question was asked and answered by an earlier theology. Two things can be learned from such a review. On the one hand, one can learn how the question must be asked, the limits within which it must be set. On the other, one can learn how to achieve the freedom necessary for asking the question. Relative to the former, I believe we can learn from our glance at medieval theology that the question of God's reality as perceived by faith must be set within the limits of the world. This question dare not be asked by looking away from the world. This should be obvious from the fact that for the Christian faith God's creation is not only man, but also the world in which man has his life according to God's will. Even though the purpose and purport of God's revelation is the salvation of man, it is impossible to conceive of this without including the salvation of the world.

Let us turn now, however, to the latter benefit to be gained from our review of medieval theology. This has to do with the freedom necessary for asking the question about the reality of faith, including liberation from the systems and the concepts used by theology in an earlier day. I hope it has become clear that the metaphysical concepts of medieval theology, despite their enviable sagacity and the admirably deep thinking that went into formulating them, have become for us unserviceable, not simply here and there but entirely. There are two reasons for this.

First, the way we live in the world, having to take the world seriously whether we want to or not, indicates that the world we live in is a different world from the one the man of the Middle Ages lived in. As I have already indicated, this change is most plainly seen in the fact that modern man considers himself responsible for the world he lives in. He is responsible for the order without which the world could not remain the kind of place in which it is possible to live meaningfully. This responsibility has fallen on man because, since the Middle Ages, he has developed modern science and the technology that accompanies it. It is important to note from the standpoint of this discussion that modern science has liberated itself from the metaphysics that dominated the thinking of both the Middle Ages and the ancient world. The change that has occurred in the relation of man to the world is not a simple matter of choice. We could not undo it if we wanted to, regardless of our grounds, for with the change man has assumed responsibility for the world. He could abandon the responsibility only at the cost of abandoning the world to chaos. On the whole, this change means that the world has become a historical world, historical in the sense that man stands over against the world as the one who is responsible for its order, responsible for its remaining a world. With this change, however, metaphysical thinking has lost the power and validity it had exerted upon the understanding of the reality of God and the world for over two thousand years.

The other reason metaphysical concepts have become unserviceable can be found within theology itself. This change occurred when Luther discovered the reality of God and his revelation in the word of God as testified to by the Bible. Since I shall later deal in some detail with the relation between word and reality, a few brief remarks are enough at this point. Before Luther's time, the Bible was read as the divine lawbook of the world. As such, the Bible could be understood and explained in terms of the metaphysical understanding of reality that lay at the foundation of medieval theology. Luther, however, recognized the Bible as the witness of the word by which God calls into being what is not (Rom. 4:17b). It is the word by which he calls men into a life to be lived "in the world but not of it." The reality of God is the kind of reality that is revealed to man in the word of God and, as Luther never tired of saying, in this word alone. If that is so, then this reality can be perceived only in faith. "God's works are his words. Doing and speaking are for him the same thing." (Weimar Ausgabe 3, 152 = Weimar edition of Luther's works, hereafter designated W.A.) And if God, as Luther says, " never has acted and never will act otherwise with men than through the word in which he promises himself to men as their God, we can have communion with him in no other way than by faith in the word of his promise " (W.A. 6, 516). Both stand together: God's promise, in which he promises himself to men as their God, and faith. Without the promise there could be no faith. Without faith the promise would be useless. Only in faith can one rely on the promise, and only in this way can the promise be fulfilled.

It is certainly clear that this faith is fundamentally different from the faith about which medieval theology speaks. We have heard that in the theology of the Middle Ages, the sacramental event of grace is completed *ex opere operato.* The sacraments are fulfilled not by the fact that one believes in them, but by the fact that they are performed. Grace is a mysterious event in and for itself. It concerns man only after the event. And man can participate in it only when he believes in it, that is, when he holds it to be true that in the action at the altar the mysterious event of transubstantiation has been completed. The event of grace, which corresponds to faith as Luther understands faith, is totally different. It occurs directly between God and man. On the one side, there is the God who in promising his grace to man promises himself. In this word, God gives himself to man as man's God, granting life and eternal blessedness. On the other side, there is the man who gives himself to God by his faith, trusting in the word in which he has received himself from God. Faith occurs between that God and that man. It simply cannot be said of this kind of faith, as it can of medieval faith, that it is only a " preparation," a *causa dispositiva,* for the reception of grace.

Of course, one could say that this kind of faith is a " subjective act of man," if one meant by it that it is man who believes. But this is an entirely different kind of " subjectivity " than is meant in medieval theology. For the faith that corresponds to the word of God, in the sense of responding to God's word, is possible only because of the creative power of the word, a power that it has precisely because it is God's word. One of Luther's remarks from his earlier period may help to clarify what is meant here. The word of God can be understood by viewing it as sacrament, for through faith the word effects what it says (W.A. 9, 442) . If one understands the gospel as sacrament in this sense, it is possible to apply the medieval formula to it and say that it happens *ex opere operato*. That means it occurs in what is said. Obviously, this event would not occur in isolation from man. It is, rather, an event that takes place immediately between God and man. It would also be quite senseless to say that it is consummated not because one believes in it but because it happens. For the happening when God speaks his word cannot be disassociated from the faith that hears. It might be noted in passing that Luther was later to understand the sacraments of Holy Communion and Baptism in this same way. To be sure, this faith is the faith of man. But it is not just man's subjective attitude toward God's word. Rather, through the word, faith is wrought in man. Gerhard Ebeling has put it well: " Faith is the effectuation of the word as that which it claims to be, namely, God's word." (*Evangelische Evangelienauslegung*, p. 382.)

My choice of medieval theology as the initial orientation for today's question about the reality of God and his revelation has had a double purpose. First, as I have indicated, a fundamental change has taken place between the general understanding of reality in the Middle Ages and our own understanding, a change that cannot be reversed. For the man of the Middle Ages, with ancient Greek metaphysics at the roots of his thinking, the real was that which has always been. To be sure, in medieval theology this no longer takes the form of the Greek concept of the eternal world of ideas, by which the Greeks sought to comprehend the cosmos as an unchanging structure. In the Middle Ages this concept of the eternal world of ideas was replaced by the concept of the realization of a plan, a plan for which the whole idealistic structure was only a tool, only an apparatus. (Compare for the following my book *Demythologizing and History,* pp. 21 ff., and my article " Das abendländische Geschichtsdenken," in *Zeitschrift für Theologie und Kirche,* 1954, pp. 280 f. and p. 331.) With the idea of the world as the realization of a plan, " God steps into history," as Dilthey says, " and directs the hearts of men toward the realization of his purpose " (Gesammelte Schriften, I, p. 330). Here we see a " grandiose theological scheme for the structure of historical life " proposed by medieval theology (*ibid.,* p. 333). The plan that God will bring about is to be found, so it was thought, in the Bible. According to this plan, mankind is seen as " a unit, an individual, who must go through the stages of life but who, because he is a pupil, must receive the rules of this development by and large from the teacher, who educates him according to a plan " (*ibid.,* p. 336). Historical facts known from tradition and from experience were incorporated " by theological interpretation " into the whole structure known from the divine plan. Without a doubt, the notion of the " whole " is the key concept in the metaphysical and hierarchical universe that medieval theology identified with the church. The whole is the one divine wisdom which, according to Augustine, contains innumerable and unlimited treasures of intelligible things, in which the invisible, unchanging sources also contain all visible and changing things. (*De civitate dei* I, c, 10: *Una sapientia, in qua sunt immensi atque infiniti thesauri rerum intelligibilium, in quibus sunt omnes invisibiles atque incommutabiles rationes rerum etiam visibilium et mutabilium.*)

nance of metaphysical thinking was considerably shaken by the Reformation, especially through the theology of Luther. But, powerful as were Luther's thrusts in the direction of a new theology, a theology no longer metaphysical in the medieval sense but historical, these beginnings could not take effect. Luther's successors hardened his theology into confessional orthodoxy too rapidly. Of course, in the long run theology could not completely seal off historical thinking. Through the influence of humanism, it came more and more into acceptance in the secular sciences. But the influence has always come from the outside and has not been worked out with regard to the particular reality that theology is concerned with. As a result, the relationship of theology to historical thinking has been a strangely divided one. In the historical disciplines, Biblical exegesis and church history, historical thinking has been practiced quite as it is practiced in secular historical sciences. Systematic theology, however, has been very reserved toward historical thinking. Because it cannot be fully ignored, attempts have been made in various ways to accomplish the impossible task of harmonizing the traditional metaphysical and the new historical thinking.

To conclude this introduction, I wish to show with the help of an example from Luther's theology what the decisive acceptance of historical thinking in theology could mean. In February, 1519, Luther was asked by George Spalatin, chaplain to the Elector of Saxony, to give the elector an exposition of John 6:37: "All that the Father gives me will come to me; and him who comes to me I will not cast out." In his exposition, Luther juxtaposes two ways of knowing God. On one side, he puts the way of the scholastic theologians who, by slipping into speculation (*in absolutas divinitatis speculationes*), have surrendered the humanity of Christ. The result is that the soul of man simply cannot stand in the presence of the sublime power, majesty, and wisdom of God. Luther himself, as he says, had been plagued most miserably and dangerously by such efforts. As an alternative, he urgently recommends another way of knowing God. Whoever would meditate and ponder over God in a wholesome way should put everything aside except the humanity of Christ. He should not stop there, however, but press farther and reflect on this: Behold, he does nothing of his own will, but he does all things by the will of the Father. At this point, the sweetest will of the Father, shown in the humanity of Christ, will begin to be pleasing. Just this is both the attracting and the giving of the Father. In this will God the Father can be surely and confidently grasped. Neglect this way of knowing the Father, and nothing remains except to fall into the eternal depths. For God does not wish man to come to him, and know him, and seek to love him in any other way than this. For, as he says, " I am the way, and the truth, and the life; no one comes to the Father, but by me." Meditate in this way, says Luther to Spalatin, and you will shortly be a deeper theologian than all the scholastics, who not only know nothing about this door and this way, but who by their imaginations and their speculative constructions also shut themselves out. (W.A. *Briefe* I, 328 f.) Luther cannot have meant that the scholastic theologians knew nothing at all of the humanity and the manhood of Christ. But they knew of this humanity — and herein lies Luther's reproach — only within the " constructions of their speculations," within the *machinis speculationum.* Thereby they have forsaken the real humanity of Christ and are left with the divinity alone. (W.A. 33, 155.) This means that in the pride of their speculative knowledge of God they had only metaphysical notions of the human and divine natures of Christ. " If, instead, one can humble oneself," suggests Luther, " and cling to the word with one's whole heart, and stay with the humanity of Christ, the divinity will indeed appear, and the Father and the Holy Spirit and the whole divinity will seize you." (W.A. 33, 156.) Contrasted with the metaphysical theology of the Middle Ages, what Luther says here about Christ's being human marks the clear beginning toward properly historical theology.

2. THE CHRISTIAN TURNING POINT

The reality that the Christian faith believes in and by which its nature as faith is determined is a man — the man Jesus of Nazareth. The reality of this man, according to this faith, is such that everything is founded on him. " All things were made through him, and without him was not anything made that was made," as the prologue to the Gospel of John says. The claim advanced by such an assertion is that divine power is at work in this man. But faith must not take its idea of the nature of the divine power from elsewhere and then apply that idea to the very man in whom it is realized. To do so would obviate a valid understanding of this man and of the nature of the faith in him. To be sure, all the New Testament concepts that are applied by faith to the man Jesus of Nazareth, such as Christ, Son of God, Lord of the World, and so on, had their origin in the history of the religions of that time. However, one would scarcely do justice to the interpretation given them by the New Testament if one did not notice that the meaning of these names has undergone a profound transformation in the process of being applied to Jesus. Previously they had referred to a being which in its intrinsic essence was heavenly and only temporarily assumed a human form. The names could be validly applied only where the divine substance was in some way obvious.

But when these concepts were transferred by the Christian faith to Jesus, they received their meaning from his humanity.

As a result of this transformation, the criterion for the genuineness of the Christian faith consists in whether faith is able to understand all it believes about this man from Nazareth in terms of the reality of his humanity. In other words, it is in Jesus' existence as a man that faith first comes to recognize what it means to be the Christ, or the Son of God. Therefore, faith is only genuinely Christian faith when it perceives the divinity of the man Jesus in his humanity, in the being that he has as a man. This is what Paul is referring to when he says that he preaches nothing but " Christ crucified, a stumbling-block to Jews and folly to Gentiles, but to those who are called, both Jews and Greeks, Christ the power of God and the wisdom of God " (I Cor. 1:23 f.; 2:2). And Paul means the " crucified Christ " when he says further that he is made by God " our wisdom, our righteousness and sanctification and redemption; therefore, as it is written, ' Let him who boasts, boast of the Lord ' " (I Cor. 1:30 f.). This message, says Paul, is the " secret wisdom of God," the " hidden wisdom " which God " decreed before the ages for our glorification," the wisdom understood by " none of the rulers of this age " (ch. 2:7 f.). In saying this about the crucified Christ, Paul could not have meant the kind of Messiah his Jewish contemporaries understood, or the kind of " savior of the world " equipped with the supernatural powers of a heavenly creature the Hellenistic " Greeks " expected. Rather, he meant the Christ that Jesus was in the humanity that his crucifixion manifested. This Christ is to be found nowhere but in Jesus' being as a man. Christ is not behind or beyond his human existence. When Paul says the power of God and the wisdom of God is the crucified Christ, he is saying that this Christ was a man, a man in his utmost humanity.

A man in his utmost humanity is a man who, in the world in which he lives, has nothing of which he can "boast." Perhaps we can better understand what Paul means by "boasting" in this familiar phrase when we see that "boasting" is the result of a man's "self-consciousness." One's self-consciousness is what one is as a "somebody" in the world. The boasting that Paul refuses is the expression of a self-consciousness achieved through attainments as the world judges them. They are achievements that bring that degree of esteem without which life cannot be lived in the world. The man who is deprived of this "boasting" and whose chances of achieving this kind of self-consciousness are destroyed, is a man repulsed, thrown back, stripped of any respect, and reduced to the sheer nakedness of his being. He is nothing in the world to which he belongs.

It is not *in spite of* his reduction to nothingness in the eyes of his world that Jesus is the Christ. He is the Christ precisely because this nothingness was his being as a man. This is what "crucified Christ" means in the exceedingly paradoxical language of the apostle. His language is paradoxical because in the most radical way it removes from the title "Christ" the meaning it traditionally had — a meaning that, incidentally, tends all too easily to become associated with the title again. But this meaning must be opposed, lest the cross be "emptied" (ch. 1:17). For it is from the cross that the title "Christ" as applied to Jesus receives its new meaning. According to this new meaning, which follows the "secret and hidden" wisdom of God, the man Jesus of Nazareth, in the sheer nakedness of his being, acting in obedience to God, took the nothingness and lostness of the whole human world upon himself as his fate, letting himself be crucified, thereby taking upon himself the curse that lay upon the world. In this deed he released the world from its curse (Gal. 3:13).

The wisdom of God in its very nature must be hidden

from the "perishing world" and its wise ones, its scribes and sophisticates, who understand the world and its wisdom. To their minds, a wisdom proclaimed in a message of a crucified Christ could only be branded as foolishness. For such a message excludes the very thing that to them guarantees life in this world, namely, the boasting, or self-consciousness, grounded in the world and in the fulfillment of the law of the world. (Rom. 3:27.) Yet it was through this message, so foolish to the worldly wise, "a fragrance from death to death" (II Cor. 2:16), that God made their wisdom into foolishness. God's wisdom, decreed before the ages, has been hidden from the perishing world, so that none of the rulers recognized the One in whom God's wisdom is realized. "For if they had, they would not have crucified the Lord of glory." (I Cor. 2:8.) Now, however, in the new age God proves himself in his wisdom and power as God to those who have nothing in the world they can boast about, to those to whom, as Paul once said, the world has been crucified, and they to the world (Gal. 6:14), to those who have been thrown back upon their stark being as man. "To *their* glory" God decreed his wisdom. For them, in contrast to the others, the message of the crucified Christ is "a fragrance from life to life" (II Cor. 2:16). Therefore, those who belong to the Christian community appear foolish in the eyes of the world, for their faith is in Jesus Christ as the One who is made wisdom and power by God for their sakes. "Not many were powerful, not many were of noble birth." Rather, they were despised and considered as nothing by the standards of the world. (I Cor. 1:26 ff.)

Paul is undoubtedly thinking here of the fact that the members of the first Christian congregations came out of the lower classes of society. But it is not their social inferiority that is decisive. It is true that their lack of respectability and their nothingness in the eyes of the world around them may have made their ears more open to the

" word of the cross." Jesus said the same of the tax collectors and harlots, the outcasts of the Jewish world. They would enter the Kingdom of Heaven before the pious, who understood themselves as respectable and " righteous " (Matt. 21:31). What is decisive, however, is that they are the ones who recognize the wisdom and power that God has revealed in the crucified Christ " to their glory." Only through this recognition could their lack of social status acquire a positive meaning, a meaning it could never have according to " this " world's wisdom. For now their understanding is oriented to the knowledge of the wisdom that God has given them through Christ crucified for their sakes. Although by virtue of their low estate and nakedness they were despised and regarded as nothing by the world, because of this very nothingness they were able to respond to the wisdom of God, the " glory " foreordained by God for them, the glory in which they now participate.

The " glory " the apostle speaks about is, first of all, the glory of God. This glory is manifested primarily in the fact that God is the One who makes the dead alive and calls into being that which is nothing (Rom. 4:17). The ultimate demonstration of this glory, valid for the whole world, was given when God in his glory raised the crucified Christ from the dead (ch. 6:4). His death was not the death of a single individual. Because it was the death of this particular man, of course, it was the death into which the whole world of man had fallen. But just as his death was not the death of one man only, so the life into which God's glory called him out of death is the life of the whole world of man. (Compare Rom. 6:1-11.) And the glory by which the man Jesus of Nazareth, in the humiliation of his death on the cross, was made " Lord and Christ " (Acts 2:36) is the glory that God has ordained for those whose faith is in this crucified Christ. It is the glory decreed before the ages and revealed in him. The wisdom of the world can permit a man to be esteemed only to the extent that in what he does and on the basis of what he does he fits into the world's expectations. Hence, it is impossible for the world to understand the wisdom of God. According to the wisdom of God, only the man who has been thrown back, stripped of any glory and reduced to the nakedness of his being, may participate in the " glory " of God.

This wisdom, therefore, cannot be expressed in words taught by men who understand only what they have from the world, only what measures up to the world's expectations. This wisdom can be expressed only in words that receive their very meaning from what God gives man in the wisdom revealed in the crucified Christ. (I Cor. 2:12 ff.)

When Paul speaks of the " word of the cross " proclaimed as the wisdom of God, he is inferring that a new epoch has replaced the old, bringing a change in man's relation to the world and to himself. This is apparent when he says that God's wisdom is hidden from the world and its rulers but that it has become manifest through the crucified Christ to those whose faith is in him. This change radically transformed both man and the world. The alteration that accompanied this turning point in history can be seen with particular clarity in the self-consciousness of man. For in the shift in the way man understands himself in his world, it becomes obvious that the transformation has affected not just one or another part of man or the world. Man and his world have both undergone a basic transformation. Of course, the language used before and after the change is the same language. The meaning it takes on, however, is quite different. One characteristic of man's self-consciousness prior to the new era was his boast of how he could achieve and secure his being in the world. He could do this because in his self-consciousness the man of the former age was aware of belonging in and to the world in which he lived. The conditions under which he

for the new era, the era inaugurated in the crucified Christ. For in the crucified Christ a question is articulated that simply cannot be answered from the world. Such a question would necessarily appear meaningless in the context of what Paul calls the "wisdom of the world," the kind of thinking for which the world is the all-embracing reality. If, however, a man can continue to hold to the question that becomes articulate in the crucified Christ, and can refuse to answer it from the world and its wisdom, he will come to realize that this question is not simply one he asks. It is asked of him. It is a question that puts him in question. This means, however, that he can answer the question only with himself. Moreover, it means that his being put in question precedes and is the origin of all his questioning. Only as he himself is put in question is it possible for man henceforth to ask about the world and his relationship to it.

3. THE ORIGIN OF THE MODERN SELF-CONSCIOUSNESS

In an essay on "The Origin of the Philosophical Self-consciousness" ("Die Herkunft des philosophischen Selbstbewusstseins," *Logos,* Internationale Zeitschrift für Philosophie der Kultur, XXXII, 1933, pp. 225 ff.), Gerhard Krüger shows what the change in the relation of man to the world and to himself signifies for Western thinking. Krüger begins with the difference between the philosophical self-consciousness of classical and of modern philosophy. The latter differs from the former in asking "not only about the world, and not only about man in so far as he belongs to the world, but initially and simultaneously about ourselves as the questioner" (*ibid.,* p. 226).

Identifying " self-consciousness " as " reflection in the fundamental philosophical sense, the reflectiveness characteristic of man as man," Krüger proposes the surprising thesis that the self-consciousness expressed in modern philosophy has its origin in " the Christian understanding of the complete powerlessness, the impotence, of man before God." Of course reflection, and with it self-consciousness, comes into existence in a naïve sense, Krüger says, wherever resistance is experienced. For when they meet opposition " the naïve drives of life are repulsed, thrown back on themselves, forcing them to know their own strength." This experience is not radical enough, however, since the " relatively naïve self-consciousness still has, or at least assumes it has, an untested store of powers in reserve." Only after the experience of total shipwreck, only after experiencing " impotence in the face of an opposing power which is overwhelming," does a " completely reflected self-consciousness " come into being. " The influence of such a completely reflected self-consciousness goes beyond the experience of the single individuals and the single areas in which opposition and impotence are met. It affects the being of man as a whole. In order for man to see through himself this thoroughly, he must encounter an unusually strong opposing force. In order for him to become aware that his whole being as man is threatened, he must feel himself hard pressed in a very crucial way." This overwhelming power which reduces man to his essential humanity Krüger believes should be sought in the experience of Christian faith. (*Ibid.*, p. 229.)

If this thesis is right, it has extraordinarily important consequences for the understanding of reality in general, but especially for the understanding of the reality with which faith and theology are concerned. It means that " we see everything as a matter of course in the light of our self-consciousness. We see things as they appear when we reflect on the act of seeing," so that " the one who sees is the presupposition of all that is seen." (*Ibid.*, p. 226.) When this is applied to the reality that concerns faith and theology, the conclusion is unavoidable that the presupposition of God's reality and revelation is the believing man.

One can well understand the apprehension that is stirred up in church circles as well as in theology by such a statement. For, to the ordinary way of thinking, it can have only one interpretation. This statement abandons what is called the " objective " ground of faith. Nothing remains of revelation but " subjective believing." Faith would then be directed no longer toward a " transcendent divine which is over against us." It could not receive a divine footing that would transcend subjectivism. Instead, faith would become an attitude immanent to man. All the more reason, one might say, for asserting the objectivity of the reality of revelation.

If Krüger's thesis is right, however, and the " completely reflected self-consciousness " in which " the one who sees is the presupposition of all that is seen " does have its origin in the " Christian understanding of the impotence of man before God," and if this self-consciousness originates in the Christian faith, then the claim that the man who has faith is the presupposition of God's reality and revelation would have its origin in the Christian faith itself. For it says nothing that does not follow as a consequence of the Christian faith. The self-consciousness of the man who experiences his impotence before God in faith is so completely reflected that he, the believer, is the presupposition of everything believed by him. To put it another way, he sees the reality of what he believes as it appears when he reflects on the faith. In order to determine whether this thesis is right, we must examine how the " Christian understanding of the impotence of man before God " can result in " the reflectedness of man." For, if it is right, the " completely reflected self-consciousness " that affects the whole being of man would correspond to man's impotence before

God experienced in the Christian faith.

This impotence has three characteristics: First, it arises where the power of God is experienced as the power of the origin from which man receives his entire existence. This is expressed in the words of Paul, " What have you that you did not receive? " (I Cor. 4:7.) Nothing that man is and has is exempt from the experience of impotence in the face of this power. In other words, this impotence is not the effect of a superior force that overpowers man from the outside. It grasps him instead in the center of his own being, where the origin is powerful in him, exerting its dominion over his whole existence in the same way the origin holds sway over him. Were it otherwise, it would be impossible to understand how, out of the experience of " opposition " by this power, a reflection could arise embracing the whole existence of man and the entire reality that concerns him, a reflection that is the complete " reflection of man's being."

The second characteristic of the impotence experienced in the face of the overwhelming divine power is that this impotence includes not just the sum of what man has received from God's power but the whole. This whole is man in his being as man. It is man himself, man in his whole selfhood, who experiences his impotence. It should be noted that this " whole," the selfhood of man, his being as man, which comes to man in the experience of impotence before God, is something that did not and could not occur prior to the era of the Christian faith. For the reflection in which the classical man was conscious of himself was a reflection that saw man " joined to his logos in the same way he and other beings belonged to the cosmos." As a result, man " did not see himself, in the strict sense of the word " (*ibid.*, p. 226) . And the whole sought by his reflection was not the whole of man but of the cosmos. For in classical thought there is only one whole, and man participates in it only as he is rightly incorporated into the order of the cosmos. Thus, it can be said of the rationality (*Nous*) of Aristotle that it "forgets itself in the observation of things; it lives in theory and is absorbed by it." Even the "Socratic-Platonic 'self-knowledge' in no sense changes this." (*Ibid.*, p. 226; compare the quotation cited by Krüger from Dilthey's *Einleitung in die Geisteswissenschaften*, Gesammelte Schriften I, pp. 178 f.: "Even to Socrates it did not occur that the phenomena of the external world correspond to man's consciousness, that in this self-consciousness a being, a reality, is given us, the knowledge of which discloses to us first and foremost an incontestable reality.") But the self-reflection occasioned by the Christian faith seeks a different "whole," the wholeness of man himself. "Man himself" is no longer man integrated into the whole of the cosmos. Instead, he is the man who stands in his wholeness over against the cosmos. He has this wholeness, to be sure, not of himself but only as he experiences it from the call of God, who calls man to himself as a whole self, the man himself. In this call the overwhelming power of God is experienced. Therefore, it is man himself in his being as man who experiences his impotence.

Following from this there is a third characteristic of the Christian understanding of man's impotence before God. Through this experience man comes to himself in an authentic sense. For only in this experience of radical impotence, from which nothing man is and has is excluded, is God recognized as the power of origin, the power that calls man into being to live as a self before God. Only in this does man come to an authentic understanding of himself. Only then does he see himself as one who has no other being than the being in responsibility to which the call of God calls him. As a result of hearing this call and of answering the responsibility to which he is called, a reflection arises that begins to "penetrate everything taken for granted" and begins to see that the possibility of this reflection is not "to be understood in the same way" as all other possibilities. The things " taken for granted " and " all the other possibilities " are those in which man, in so far as he belongs to the world and can understand himself in terms of the world, is competent. Only by the reflection in responsibility to God's call is man able to " measure the limits of his own power " (Krüger, *op. cit.*, p. 229) . From the standpoint of faith, it is crucial that he not evade the responsibility to which he has been called. It is a responsibility that he is able to fulfill only with himself, just as he can answer the call only with himself. He must not allow himself to think he can fulfill it by substituting the doing of just " this or that."

This reflection, therefore, is not something that is added subsequent to faith. It is faith itself. It is the reflection of faith when Paul says, for example, " We hold that man is justified by faith apart from the works of law " (Rom. 3:28) . For in thinking and confessing this, Paul gives himself unconditionally in his whole existence to the responsibility in which he stands before God. He stands before God in the only way it is possible to stand, as one who has his being in response, as one who is responsible. The only authentic " work " of faith is that it stands constant in this reflection. This work consists of nothing more nor less than man's being himself before God. This of course is a work which, unlike other works, man cannot complete in his own power. For the self-consciousness in which he is aware of himself has its ground not in him but solely and uniquely in the call in which he knows he is called. There is no other possibility, therefore, of his remaining constant in this call and thus of being before God in his being except as he remains constant in hearing this call. To remain constant in hearing is what it means to believe. The " things previously taken for granted," once they are penetrated by reflection and thereby incorporated into the impotence before God, are seen for what they are: " works of the law." Through the works of the law man at one time supposed he could rise above the multiplicity of little experiences of impotence in the world and could stand before God with his " treasury of merits." The reflection of faith, however, is so enveloping and so penetrating that under its light the " treasury " melts away.

4. THE CHRISTIAN'S RELATION TO THE WORLD

An adequate understanding of self-consciousness should take into consideration man's relation to the world. In the previous discussion I indicated that self-consciousness originates in the reflection of faith that calls a man to himself. I indicated that the whole sought in this reflection is not the world as given in the self-consciousness of the pre-Christian man. It is man himself, man in his selfhood. That means that by this reflection the relationship of man to the world also becomes fundamentally different. For the pre-Christian man the cosmos is the ultimate, all-embracing reality. Its eternal order is the fundamental problem. The decisive issue for man, therefore, is both *that* and *how* he may adapt himself and his actions to this order. His piety consists in the worship of the order and of the powers that support it. For the Christian man, however, this piety undergoes a basic change. The profound change in the relation of man to himself and to the world brought about by the advent of Christianity is nowhere more clearly exemplified than in the writings of Paul. Paul identifies pre-Christian piety, with its reverent worship of the gods who uphold the eternal order of the world, as that godlessness and wickedness with which men suppress the truth (Rom. 1:18). What took place and what continues to take place in that worship seems now, in the light of the knowledge of faith, to be a monstrous perversion. In this piety the world and its powers, regarded by faith as God's creatures, take the place of the Creator and receive the honor that belongs to the Creator alone (Rom. 1:23 ff.). This perversion has still another consequence that affects man and his nature. The worship of the creation instead of the Creator means simply that one understands himself in terms of the creature. Understanding himself in terms of the world and its powers, he falls into the hands of these powers. These powers have a kind of law. They maintain the order of the world. For man to conceive himself in their terms means for him to trust them as the guardians of his life. If he would save his life, he must fulfill their law.

One can hardly regard that piety too deeply and must constantly be reminded that the world as it appears here is a religious reality. As here conceived and experienced it seems to be surrounded by a powerful mystery that prevails wherever the gods are involved. Thus, in the New Testament passages where the world seems in contradiction to God and his revelation, and where believers are warned not to "be conformed to the world" (Rom. 12:2), or where Paul confesses that through Christ the world has been crucified to him and he to the world (Gal. 6:14), the concept of the world is a religious concept. It is not the moral concept used in most popular and pious discourse. Likewise, the world is a religious notion when it receives the adoration that is due the Creator. Now if one is clear about this, he can also understand the profound and all-embracing attachment by which the pre-Christian man is bound to the world and its powers. Hence, he can also appreciate the freedom from the world that the Christian man achieved through the gospel of Jesus Christ. Only in this way can he judge how thoroughgoing and comprehensive was the repentance, the *metanoia,* that accompanied faith in the Christian preaching. This *metanoia* was just as deeply felt by the contemporary Jew as it was by the so-called pagan, the non-Jew, the Gentile, as he is designated by Paul, who, with the rest of the Bible, does not know the word "pagan." For Paul charges that the Jews as well as the Gentiles have substituted false gods for their Creator. By their legalism they have exchanged the creature for the Creator; they have substituted for the Creator of the world the world created by their piety and constituted by the law they worship.

Freedom from the world and its powers is accessible to the Christian man through the gospel of Jesus Christ. To comprehend this freedom in all its meaning, one must understand the enormity of the pre-Christian piety. The world from which the Christian has been set free is conceived religiously and not simply in moral terms. Hence, this freedom is also a religious concept. To be sure, it has the greatest moral consequences. But neither the consequences nor the freedom from which they stem are correctly estimated until one understands the foundation of this freedom. As one can easily see, this freedom is not rooted in the enlightenment and the profanation of the world that commenced in the enlightenment — a profanation that in the Hellenistic period was one of the final results of Greek philosophy. Neither, however, is it based in the purely negative opposition to the religious worship of the world and its powers, as it occurred so impressively in Hellenistic Gnosticism. Here the conception of the world becomes "an emphatically negative idea. As such it has greater emotional appeal and so is perhaps more decisive than it was previously as a concept of positive value." "The sublime unity of the cosmos and God is broken asunder. A monstrous abyss is opened up which is never again fully overcome: God and world, God and nature, are separated, become alien to each other and contradictory." (Hans Jonas, *Gnosis und antiker Geist,* pp. 148 f.) The result is a pessimism with regard to the world, or nihilism, which " certainly in distinction from the Indian type conceives the world not as the absolute lack of being of a pure nothingness but rather as something real and decidedly substantial, and as an object of an equally decided hate." The profaned world thus becomes religiously specific by the complete contrast of this dualism. Indeed, it becomes religiously powerful in a way as intensive as it is paradoxical. For it is " darkness and death " in a thoroughly substantial opposition to the heavenly " light and life " (*ibid.*, p. 150). These Gnostic perspectives achieved their greatest effectiveness in the early church, primarily through Marcion, who connected them with the Christian faith in a suggestive way, since he understood this faith and man's freedom from the world that was bound up with it. The traces of this view are still discernible today in the preaching and theology of the church. Accordingly, one usually understands the repeated warning of the New Testament writers to " watch " and " stand fast " in the freedom of the faith in the sense of an ascetic detachment from the world. Such a view of freedom is certainly appropriate to a world conceived as hostile and in contradiction to God, as Gnostic dualism conceived it.

As a matter of fact, there are in the New Testament, in particular in the Pauline and Johannine literature, numerous seemingly dualistic statements about two worlds. Taken out of context, if they do not fully suggest it, they certainly do encourage such a Gnostic understanding of the world. The harsh contradictions as they appear between God and world, flesh and spirit, and in numerous other ways, have always fostered the view that the thinking of the New Testament writers is dominated by the dualism of two worlds — a material-sense world, inimical and opposed to God, and a spiritual world, ruled by and filled with God. Man would live in that material world of sense as in a prison and separated from God. For this viewpoint says that sin would rule in the world because the world is the world of flesh. It is easy to understand that this conception gained a foothold in the Christian community. For the form of thinking at that time was mythical. It dealt with a battle of two worlds, which is cosmic in scope. This mythical form of thinking seemed then, as it does even today, the appropriate way of explaining the change in the whole being of the world and man that occurred in the advent of Jesus Christ.

This kind of thinking proceeds from the world, or better, from both the enemy worlds, or aeons, that are in conflict with each other. These worlds are the true subjects in the conflict ensuing between them, and the conflict is a cosmic process. Consequently, man is hardly more than an object drawn into the process because he shares substantially in both worlds. According to the cosmological myth, the material-sense world arose by a fall from the God of light. Man, who originally belonged to the world of light, is dragged into this material world by the pretemporal Fall. The one thing necessary for man is to arrive at the proper understanding of the event of his salvation through the world of light. This understanding enables him to join the right side and detach himself from all that belongs to the earthly world. Thus he participates in the salvation that occurs in this process of the world. The necessary knowledge is given him by the Savior sent from the world of light to the earthly world. At the same time, the Savior establishes sacramental rites through which man is cleansed from the earthly matter that clings to him, and by which his original spiritual form is strengthened.

Although the New Testament writers approach the Gnostic view by use of concepts in part borrowed from the Gnostics, their thinking is quite different. Unlike the Gnostics, their thinking does not begin with the world. It begins wholly with man and his relation to God. When the New Testament writers speak of the world in the negative sense, as they frequently do, they refer to it as " this " world. But in that case it is the world as subjected to nothingness and decay through the sin of man and not through cosmic fate. For the New Testament writers, therefore, there are not two worlds, but only one, the world created by God. This *one* divine world is the world that man's sin has turned into a fundamentally perverted being. The sin of man is exchanging the Creator for the creature by trusting in the life available to the " flesh " and giving the world, which is God's creature, the glory belonging to its Creator. Consequently, the fundamental order of all being, namely, the being of the Creator and the creature, is violated. As the world which is God's creation is turned into the fallen world of nothingness, man is changed into a perverted being. The fundamental order of being is violated because the worship of the creature instead of the Creator means nothing more nor less than that man understands himself in terms of the creature, that is, from the standpoint of the world and its powers instead of in terms of the Creator. Consequently, man falls under the authority of these powers. For they are of a lawful kind. They preserve the order of the world. To understand oneself in terms of such powers means, therefore, to trust in them as if one lived under their protection. Whoever will preserve his life must fulfill their laws. With this trust in the laws of the world, however, man has forfeited his freedom. He has forfeited not only his freedom in his relation to the world. What is more decisive is that he has forfeited his freedom in his relation to God.

Now, for a proper understanding of what the New Testament writers say negatively about the world, we must realize that it is man's forfeited freedom for God that has made the world what it is for him now. It is this freedom which shall be granted him anew through faith in Jesus Christ. We could just as well say that the negative statements of the New Testament about the world must be understood from faith. For in faith we are given not only new freedom for God but also new freedom from the world. These statements refer to the world recognized by faith as the world as it is before the coming of faith. It is the world that had fallen into nothingness through man's sin. To understand these statements correctly, it is necessary to be clear about the nature of the freedom that is newly available in faith.

5. THE FREEDOM OF FAITH

What kind of freedom is the freedom of faith? This can be seen most clearly in the fact that Paul applies to freedom the same word he uses for the majesty and deity of God. He speaks of the "doxa," or the "glory," of the freedom of the sons of God (Rom. 8:21). In this concept of glory Paul implies "power," the "power" with which God demonstrates his divine nature by giving life to the dead (ch. 4:17). Whatever can be said about the "dynamis" of God, his divine power, is also true of his "doxa," or "glory." It is this glory by which Christ was raised from the dead (ch. 6:4). In the third chapter of Second Corinthians, Paul speaks extensively of the effect this "doxa" has on those who believe in Christ, who was resurrected from the dead by means of this glory. Here Paul contrasts the "dispensation of the Spirit" with that of the "letter," meaning "the dispensation of the law." In order to show the effect the dispensation of the "law" has on man, Paul uses the story from Exodus (Ex. 34:29 ff.) in which Moses covered his face with a veil as he proclaimed to the people the law he had received from God on Sinai. When the Jews saw the reflection of God on his face, they were afraid to come near him. Then Paul interprets this narrative in terms of his understanding of the law. It means that the Jews were " hardened " as a result of the law and the " glory " laid upon it. Therefore, they did not recognize that the " glory " of the law that was mediated through Moses and " carved in letters " was only a fading glory. As a result, however, knowledge of the true " glory " of God remains hidden to them. That is the reason why " to this day whenever Moses is read a veil lies over their minds " (II Cor. 3:15). Paul then quotes the sentence from the Old Testament narrative: " Whenever Moses went in before the Lord to speak with him, he took the veil off " (Ex. 34:34) with which he had hidden his face from the people, because the reflection of God's glory was upon it. However, Paul now applies this statement, not to Moses, but to those who by faith in Jesus Christ turn away from the law to Christ as their Lord. Paul's thought is that the Jews are held in the captivity of their hearts under the Mosaic law and its " dispensation of the letter," or, as he also calls it here, " the dispensation of damnation." In spite of all their obedience to the law, they cannot be free for God. They are held in bondage by the " letter " of the law and are estranged from God, which is damnation. To the bondage of the heart, hardened and deadened by the letter of the law, Paul now contrasts the freedom of the Spirit, who opens our hearts and makes them alive. For this purpose he uses the illustration of a mirror in which one recognizes himself when he looks into it " with unveiled face." The mirror serves as an illustration of the " glory," or the " doxa," of the Lord. Hence, he says, " We all " — that is, the congregation of believers — " with unveiled face, beholding the glory of the Lord as in a mirror, are being changed into his likeness from glory to glory." (II Cor. 3:18.)

In order to understand this sentence, one must know, first of all, what is meant by the concept of " glory." It has a much more exact and profound meaning here than it does in popular use. That is most clearly shown by the fact that it is used by Paul primarily when he is referring to the resurrection of the dead, and especially the resurrection of the crucified Christ. Thus he says the resurrection of Christ takes place through the "glory of the Father" (Rom. 6:4). This "glory" of God is the power of calling into being "the things that do not exist" (ch. 4:17). This power God, the Lord, has, "from whom and through whom and to whom are all things. To him be glory forever" (ch. 11:36). It is, therefore, the power by which God gives life to the dead and justifies the ungodly (ch. 4:17 and ch. 5), or it is, as Paul also says, the power of God which is made perfect in the weakness of men (II Cor. 12:9). All of this shows that it is the true divine power, for through it the "one God, the Father, from whom are all things and for whom we exist," distinguishes himself from the many so-called gods and lords, of whom, as Paul explicitly says, there are many, whether it be in heaven or on earth (I Cor. 8:5 f.).

However, these "by nature are no gods" (Gal. 4:8). Those also share in this "glory," therefore, who are brought to life and made righteous by it, for they live and are what they are wholly and completely as a result of this glory. Therefore, it can be said of them also that they are "glorified" (Rom. 8:30). That is true, above everything else, of him whose entire being was supported by this glory, and who, therefore, has become the revelation of this glory. And when it is said in this passage that he is the "Lord of glory," this means that he is the Lord through this "glory" of God. Through him and through his Lordship, however, those who acknowledge him as their Lord also share in this glory, just as those who suffer with him will also be "glorified" with him (ch. 8:17).

Recall, then, the Old Testament narrative concerning the Jews who were afraid of the reflection of "glory" upon the face of Moses and whose hearts were closed by this fear of God. Paul says that in contrast to them the believers in Christ look on the " glory of the Lord " " with unveiled face." We must not overlook the fact that the references to " the mirror " and to " beholding with an unveiled face " are meant symbolically. The passage to which this sentence is the conclusion shows unmistakably that the reference to " beholding " is conditioned by the symbol of the mirror. Paul is really speaking here of something he refers to in the same passage as " confidence " (II Cor. 3:4), a " hope " by which " we are very bold " (v. 12), and finally, as he comes to the summation of his thought, the " freedom," which is the " Spirit of the Lord " (v. 17).

The " glory " Paul is referring to here is God's " eternal power and deity " (Rom. 1:20). With it he calls into being " the things that do not exist " (ch. 4:17). In that light it is clear, first of all, that the word " image," by which Paul's word *eikon* is usually translated, must be understood in the sense of a " form." A " form," moreover, receives its existence and its being completely and solely from that glory, and is what it is always as a result of the divinely creative power of this " glory." It is never what it is by its own power. It exists only in so far as it is always created anew. Thus, man, as the form of this " glory," is not an image of this " glory " sustained for itself. He is this form only in the respect that through that glory he is being eternally created, as the apostle says, " from glory to glory." We said before that those share in this " glory " who are brought to life and made righteous by it. That must be taken to mean that this glory never becomes something like a quality of man that he should or could have in and for himself. It remains, rather, the " glory " of God. However, the same glory man is made to share in raised Christ from the dead (ch. 6:4). If we keep in mind further what is meant by this " glory " of God, it is clear that the " unveiling of the face " by which the " glory of the Lord " is seen " as in a mirror " (or, without using the analogy, the freedom in which this " glory " is perceived) is not an unveiling that man has in and for himself and that he, in this and every case, brings with him to this experience. This freedom (or, using the analogy, " the unveiling of the face ") is made possible by the glory of the Lord. The being of Him who is changed into the form of this " glory " is brought about in and with this freedom.

In what has been said thus far, the relation of man to God is described as it is included and understood in the Christian faith. Three things are decisive for the concept of freedom derived in this way: First, man receives his being before God by this freedom, and he never has it except in this freedom. Freedom is not merely like a faculty that is accidental to his essence. In this freedom man is himself. Therefore, in it man has his being as a grant from God. Indeed, he has it in the sense that in this freedom he belongs to God as one who is " by God, in the sight of God " (II Cor. 2:17). This freedom, therefore, is no more his own work than his own being is. Man is so originally in freedom that it is his authentic being. In it everything else that may be said about man has its meaning. If he loses his freedom, he loses himself.

Our concern is to say something here that in essence is infinitely simple. For man is that being who, as ordinary thinking rightly assumes, does not exist in and for himself. Instead, he can fulfill himself only in so far as he can find the being to which he responds. The verb " respond " is used in the sense given it by its original Latin, *spondere,* " to pledge one's word " and by this word himself. In this sense one can fully respond only to one who addresses him. And he can " re-spond " in the full sense of the word only when his own speech permits him to be grounded in the speech of the other. If this is true of everyday speech and re-sponding, as it is practiced in discussions regardless of the topic or the partners involved, it is certainly true of conversation in which not just any old subject is broached but where the subject of the discussion is man himself, and where he is the subject in such a way that he promises himself to the other. This occurs, for example, in the language of love. Here the being of a man speaks. One can respond to such speech only with one's being. In this response a man is freely " for the other " with his being. In the freedom of the response grounded in the promise of the other, he receives from this word his being-in-relation to the other. It is in this sense that man, in the freedom for God, receives his being from God.

The same thing is meant when Paul in other places in his letters characterizes this freedom of man for God as the freedom of a son or as the " spirit of sonship " (Rom. 8:15) or simply as " sonship " (Gal. 4:5). For the " son " is the one who receives his being from his father and responds to the fatherly promise in the freedom of receiving himself. In this freedom as son, he has a share in the being of the father and he receives his being-as-son from the father's being-as-father. As Paul says: " All who are led by the Spirit of God are sons of God. For you did not receive the spirit of slavery to fall back into fear, but you have received the spirit of sonship. When we cry, ' Abba! Father! ' it is the Spirit himself bearing witness with our spirit that we are sons of God." (Rom. 8:14 ff.) How shall one correctly understand the apostle's assertion that man is the son of God? Only by attempting to understand the notion in the light of its entire background of meaning. It is not enough to understand it psychologically. One must understand these conceptions as referring to man's being as grounded in God's deity. If we cry to God in the spirit of sonship, using the name " Father," as the apostle Paul says, it is the cry of those " who are led by the Spirit of God " (Rom. 8:14 ff.). It is the answer evoked by the promise of God. It is the response. In this answer our being as freedom for God has become vocal, and we as sons respond with our being to God as Father. The promise of God on which all such filial response can be based is his word calling into being what does not exist. As Paul says, God's Spirit as Father witnesses with our spirit as sons, and thus we are called sons of God (v. 16). By this call, God promises himself to man as Father and through this promise creates a man who can be before him in the freedom of a son.

The freedom of man for God as the freedom of a son is, then, the first decisive mark of Christian freedom. The second decisive mark is that this freedom does not exist except in the knowledge of the One for whom a man is free. One can have this knowledge only while one is permitting it to be given to him and while one is receiving it from the One who discloses it to him. And since one has as little claim to freedom as one does to the being one receives by it, the knowledge about it and about Him who gives it can only be by faith. This freedom, then, is not the freedom we associate with free decision or the power over something. It means being opened, being unlocked to another person. And if the knowledge about it can only be the knowledge of faith, then faith in this sense is not a mere idea one could form of such a freedom. Nor is faith the arbitrary or emotional assumption that one has such a freedom. Faith is always an act of obedience, an act of trust in the One for whom one is free. On the basis of what has been acknowledged up to this point, we can say that this freedom is accomplished in that essential response about which we have spoken.

As we have seen, this response can be accomplished only if one is spoken to and listens. The response that faith requires is of such a sort that it must be made with the whole being, for the call to which one is obliged to respond invokes one's whole being. There can be a knowledge of this call, therefore, only in and with the true response. Any effort to know the calling in some other way, such as attempting to know what it is before responding to it, would not do justice to Him and His calling, but would hopelessly fail Him. For in that case one could not know of the other as the One who calls him into being. He would know Him instead from the standpoint of one who already intends to have his being independently of the other. Such a knowledge, however, as long as I persist in it, is unsuited and unfit for the response. For it is only in the response that I can know Him in such a way as to do justice to Him. I would like to respond to Him in the way that my presumed knowledge of Him dictates. But in the attempt, I would hopelessly fail Him.

A knowledge of God would be a knowledge in which I genuinely do justice to him and to the calling with which he calls me out of nothing into being, and to which I respond with my very being. Such knowledge is possible only as I know myself free for him in the freedom that I receive as given to me by him. The faith Paul speaks about is of a sort that in it I know myself to be free for God. Only for that reason can Paul assert that man will be justified by faith alone, " apart from works of law " (ch. 3:28).

If the being of a man is what responds to God in the freedom for him, a man can have his righteousness before God only as his being is purely conceived in this freedom. The demand of which I become aware in the freedom for God is, therefore, that I shall live my life in the obedient knowledge of the conception of my being before God. That knowledge alone justifies. It means that I shall live in the knowledge of my freedom for God. If I know of God in this way, then I also know that all other ways of knowing God can only result in denying myself the glory and deity of God that " makes alive."

We said earlier that man's freedom for God is founded in the Father's promise in which God as Father promises himself to man. In other words, man's freedom as son is founded in the freedom in which God as Father sets him free. For man as son is the image of God. Made after his likeness, he should belong to God in freedom (Gen. 1:26). By the same word in which God gives man responsibility for ruling the world, he sets him free: "Be fruitful and multiply, and fill the earth and subdue it; and have dominion over the fish of the sea and over the birds of the air and over every living thing that moves upon the earth." (V. 28.)

That marks the third point that is decisive for the concept of man's freedom for God. In the two passages in which Paul discusses the gift of the spirit of sonship, he means the freedom of the son. Following each of these passages he immediately adds that as sons we are also heirs (Rom. 8:17 and Gal. 4:1). That is not accidental. The connection of these passages makes it clear that the inheritance Paul refers to is the world. I cite only Rom. 8:17, which says that we are sons of God, and if sons, "then heirs, heirs of God and fellow heirs with Christ." The divine inheritance of Christ is the world. We have inherited it along with him. If the world is on loan to man as his inheritance, then, as Paul would say, man is a mature son, independent of the world. He is no longer subjugated to "the elemental spirits of the universe," as the heir in the order of the earthly world is who, not yet of age, is placed under guardians and tutors retained by his father. Master of all things, he is yet no different from a slave. What is meant by "the elemental spirits of the universe" becomes clear when it is seen that Paul here uses the concept of "law" and the concept of "beings that by nature are no gods" as synonyms for the elemental spirits (Gal. 4:3; compare vs. 5 and 8). It is obvious, therefore, that the reference here is to those powers to whom the pre-Christian man offered the worship and service that he owed to God. With the knowledge that the world is granted to the man who has come of age as an inheritance, the relation of man to the world is fundamentally changed. The world no longer rules him. He has become its master.

6. THE WORLD AS AN INHERITANCE

The Christian man has become master of the world. That is not all. Something infinitely deeper has happened. The freedom of the son became a possibility only with man's independence of the world and with his responsibility for it. Only in this freedom is he able to respond to God as father. This response has two inseparable meanings. First, the son is what he is from the father. Secondly, he would not really be a son if he were not independent. For, in distinction from the child, the son who has come of age belongs to the father under conditions of freedom. In the same way, man as son receives himself from the fatherly promise of God and at the same time gives himself to God in the being that belongs to him as a mature son. Without such independence, he would not be a son. But he receives the possibility of this independence at the same time as the world is given him as his inheritance. For in order to be able to respond to another in the proper sense, that is, with one's own genuine promise, he must have a world of his own. He must be independently and responsibly engaged with it as one who holds and justifies his own being. In this independence in which the filial freedom for God is possible, the full meaning of the inheritance becomes understandable for the first time as a world turned over to man.

It is not enough at this point to cite the word from Genesis with which God gives man lordship over the world. This word carries only the connotation of man's relation to the world. By contrast, the word about the inheritance refers at the same time to man's relation to the world and to his relation to God. For an inheritance is not simply a possession like any other piece of property. Something is bestowed along with it that transcends mere possession. A possession becomes an inheritance only as the testator who has given it to him on trust is and remains present to the heir. In so far as the possession is an inheritance it is and remains the enduring bond of the testator with the heir. Beyond everything that the administration of a possession may mean, administration of an inheritance means that the enduring presence of the testator has to be preserved and safeguarded by the heir. As for the inheritance by which the world is vested by God with man, this enduring presence is twofold. First, it is God's creatorhood, and secondly, his fatherhood. The former refers to the world; the latter, to man.

That God is the creator of the world does not simply mean that at some time or other he once created it and that it now exists of and in itself as he created it. What is called " world " is an ordered and meaningful whole. If the Christian faith believes that God is the creator of the world, that simply means, above all, that the world has its wholeness, its very being as world, singly and entirely, in the creatorhood of God. The world is and remains a world only in the respect that God is present in it as in his creation with his creatorhood. Hence, it can be a world to man only in this unique sense if he " clearly perceives " in it the " invisible nature, namely, his eternal power and deity " (Rom. 1:20) as God is present with it in the world. One must realize that it is this " eternal power and deity " whereby God proves he is God by nature, calling into being " the things that do not exist " (ch. 4:17). One will then understand why one must " clearly perceive " the nature of this " eternal power and deity." For the power itself makes man's awareness of it possible. " Awareness " in this sense is known in our language as the way we have of saying one is aware of his office as judge or father. That does not simply mean that the judge or father knows what he has to do or even that he does it. The expression, rather, refers to something presupposed in both. Whoever is aware of his office in the full sense of this word is aware not only of the skill his office requires in and for itself. Rather, he receives an existence in this awareness, conferred on him entirely through the office and unavailable outside his office. He validates this existence in doing what belongs to him with it, such as in acting as judge or father.

In this original and proper sense of the word one must understand the " awareness " of the eternal power and deity in which alone the world can be known as world. This awareness is possible since the world was created through the work of the creation, and it must be understood in a double way. It must be understood as the awareness of God's creatorhood in relation to the world as well as his fatherhood in relation to man. The awareness of the one is tied in the strictest sense to the awareness of the other. For God's creatorhood refers to the world as the inheritance vested with the son and as that which the heir shall administer as God's creation. On the other side, God's creatorhood as well as his fatherhood refers to man as the one to whom is given along with the world the possibility of living in the freedom for God that is the son's freedom for the father.

7. FORFEITED SONSHIP AND THE WORLD'S NOTHINGNESS

It was necessary to speak in detail of man's freedom as son in order to clarify one thing. The world which is God's creation was subjected to the " bondage of nothingness " through the forfeiture of this freedom. That makes the opposite understandable. Through the disclosure of men as God's sons, and through the new gift of freedom that is coming to them, the world can be delivered from its bondage. (Rom. 8:20 f.) On the other hand, both claims are understandable only when it is recognized that the world is not some kind of barrier between God and man from which man must free himself to come into a right relation to God. The world originally belongs in the God relation, indeed, in its very center, which is to say, in the freedom for God. Only thus does one do justice to the Christian faith, which was always faith in creation. Dualism was and still is Christianity's most dangerous heresy. Hellenistic Gnosticism formed the heresy most impressively in its concept of the world as a reality hostile to God. But unless the world is understood as the divine inheritance granted to man, man's relation to God as the Christian faith understands it is not at all possible. The Christian faith understands this relation as freedom in which man responds to God with his entire being. Such an essential response, denoted in the Bible (and not by Paul alone) as the response of son to father, is possible only in a man's independence to assert what is his own and to remain responsible for it. This independence, or, as Paul calls it, this mature sonship (Gal. 4:1 ff.), God gives to man in giving the world over to him as his inheritance. We can also say that God sets man free. God wants man to belong to him in the freedom of sonship. Sonship is the creaturehood peculiar to man in distinction from all other creatures, and has been given him as his meaning. Man is the creature who has his own world for which he is responsible and in relation to which he is independent. Only such a creature can belong to another in freedom.

There is an unequivocal result from all that has been said up to this point. The independence God bestows on man in giving him the world as his inheritance has its meaning solely in man's freedom for God. This freedom is possible through the inheritance. In his freedom man belongs to God as his son, and he is all he is " by God, in the sight of God " (II Cor. 2:17). The son in turn preserves the creative presence of God in the world in administering the inheritance of sonship bestowed on him. However, the independence would be genuine and the maturity liberating only on one condition. Just as man is given the possibility of responding to God with his entire being, so he must be given the alternate possibility of rejecting God.

The New Testament writers regard pre-Christian piety as just such a rejection of God. Paul, for example, says in the beginning of his Letter to the Romans that " the righteousness of God," which comes " through faith for faith," having been revealed in the gospel of Jesus Christ, has also been revealed as " the wrath of God . . . against all ungodliness and wickedness of men " (ch. 1:17-18). Paul means to characterize the pre-Christian piety by this ungodliness. At the same time, Paul says that with this ungodliness and wickedness men have " suppressed the truth " by their wickedness. That does not mean the sonship no longer exists. Nor does it mean that in the complex of the relations of man with God and the world something else entered here or there in place of what previously was there. Rather, everything has remained as it was. The change that has occurred is too extensive and profound to be comprehended in this way. Utterly everything has changed fundamentally, and nothing is what it was originally.

We can express this difference succinctly by saying that man in rejecting the promise of God forfeits his sonship. Moreover, what someone forfeits is not simply lost. The thing forfeited now clings to him inseparably in its fundamental perversion. It is the essence of something forfeited that it cannot be recovered again, and that it cannot be changed back into its original essence. One can forfeit only what by its nature can only be given him. If man forfeits his sonship by rejecting the promise of God, the perversion influences the distortion of the promise of God. It affects everything grounded in this promise, without exception, even the distortion of the world as the inheritance from the divine Father. The world and the inheritance become fundamentally perverted. This means that the fatherly, creative promise of God calling into being what was not has become the annihilating voice of the hidden God conjuring up the nothingness. That promise originated in the eternal source of all being, and made this original life master in all and over all that is. This voice which first sounded with such originating power sounds now in the echo of a nothingness that penetrates everything that was and is and is to be. The spirit of sonship in which we cry, "Abba! Father!" has become the servile spirit of fear (Rom. 8:15) in which, as Paul says, the law reigns as the agency of corruption and death (II Cor. 3:7 ff.).

The freedom and responsibility man has in relation to the world is threatened by this agency of nothingness and death and has ceased therefore to be free in its deepest ground. Since that has occurred, there lies upon man the unavoidable compulsion and burden of securing a space he is still able to live in. The world must now help him do this. In this way the powers of the world and their lawfulness gain the highest authority over him. He imagines they have the power to protect life. Piety, faith, and obedience must all be ruled by the powers of the world and must serve them. Man now has his self-consciousness in and from the piety in which the world is entirely governed by the powers of the law. Employing the paradigm of the Jewish religion of law, Paul calls this his "boast." By the service he devotes to these powers, man believes he can overcome the nothingness that permanently threatens him. The consequence is that he is not even able to detect that everything he does in this way only causes him to fall deeper and more hopelessly into that nothingness. For by forfeiting his sonship the son also forfeits his inheritance. Not that the inheritance, which is the world, would simply be taken away from him. Rather, it would be fundamentally perverted.

All the negative assertions that the Christian faith makes about the world must now be understood from the standpoint of this idea. Man has forfeited his sonship by the very independence that made it possible. Thereby the inheritance of the world is forfeited, the world given him by God that he might live in it in the freedom of a " son " while administering it as the creation of God. That means the idea that the world is God's creation and as such is the inheritance God has bestowed on man may on no account be abandoned. For with the forfeiture of his sonship man has also forfeited his inheritance. As a result, the inheritance is fundamentally perverted. The essence of the inheritance is that in it, in the world, God's creatorhood is present, with his invisible nature, his eternal power and deity. Man should be aware of that presence.

When one forfeits his honor, it thereafter clings inseparably to him in its fundamental perversion as dishonor. It destines his entire life because he lives at present in the sphere in which honor is valued. As one stigmatized by dishonor he can do nothing to restore his honor again unless it is given him anew. Just so, to one who forfeits his divine inheritance, the enduring and perceptible creatorhood of God changes into what Paul calls the world fallen into the nothingness and slavery of decay (Rom. 8:20 ff.). But if I may say so, this " nothingness " and " decay " is by no means the decay that is obvious and immediately perceptible. In Rom., ch. 1, where Paul speaks about it in some detail, he gives as its cause the exchange of " the glory of the immortal God for images resembling mortal man or birds or animals or reptiles " (v. 23). And they have brought about this exchange because those who executed it and who " knew God did not honor him as God or give thanks to him." Thus they " became futile in their thinking and their senseless minds were darkened. Claiming to be wise, they became fools." The " nothingness " into which their thought fell is the world in which they are no longer aware of the continuing creatorhood of God. Therefore they no longer worship God as God, as the creator. Instead of worshiping him, they worshiped the creatures deprived of their creator.

But one does not understand this " perversion " in its entire sweep and the worship allied with it if one does not also recognize that the " nothingness " and " decay " into which both man and the world have fallen is still more general and profound than has been indicated up to now. That is quite clear in Paul's statement that in the worship of the creature the truth of God is exchanged for a lie and that the creature is worshiped, not as creature, but as God and gods. This worship now asserts itself as the truth, that is, as the true worship of God. According to Paul, this " exchange of the Creator for the creature " is the real sin of man. Through it the divine inheritance, the world created by God, has been perverted into the world fallen into the nothingness and slavery of decay.

To understand what this means, one needs the help of the concept that is the real name for " nothingness " and " decay " in the theology of Paul — the concept of the " flesh." Along with that, one must also use the concept of the " law," so closely bound up with " flesh " in Paul's thought. Otherwise, it is completely unintelligible how the perversion of being into its opposite, which takes place in this exchange, engulfs the whole world and can never be abrogated. " Flesh " usually has the same meaning for Paul that it has in the Old Testament. First of all, he uses it to designate human life as it is lived, perceived by sense and amenable to human action. Therefore, in its basic meaning it is life as given in man's immediate awareness. It is life as man " has " it in being alive in the flesh.

The concept of " flesh " has a more comprehensive

meaning, however. Paul uses it to mean both the world and the things in it, in so far as these provide the space and the conditions for life as it is directly (*phanerō*) accessible to man and at his disposal in his intercourse with the world and the things in it. " Flesh " means in this more comprehensive sense not only man's sensual pursuit of life but even the moral life, and in a certain sense the religious life, too, as this is lived within the world and according to the world's law. So Paul says of Jesus that he is of David's lineage " according to the flesh " (Rom. 1:3). Paul himself, " according to the flesh " — and here that also means " according to the order of the Jewish world " — was " circumcised on the eighth day, of the people of Israel, of the tribe of Benjamin, a Hebrew born of Hebrews " (Phil. 3:5 f.). The concept of the flesh, then, like the concept of the world, does not denote something sinful in itself and opposed to God.

The concept of " flesh " also refers to the quick and sudden corruptibility and perishableness of everything that is alive after the manner of the " flesh." This is the meaning, for example, in Isa. 40:6: " All flesh is grass, and all its beauty is like the flower of the field. The grass withers, the flower fades." Man, however, by keeping certain precepts that he knows from practical experience, has the capacity to preserve a certain degree of life and forestall his eclipse. And just as worldly wisdom teaches him to be intent on the " flesh " and its life, so it teaches him the same concern in relation to everything that is named by this concept. For he knows that the things of the world perish like the flesh. It is one of the deeply ingrained and universal peculiarities of man's being, however, that he places his trust in this " flesh." Naturally so, for in it, one might say, he has his life in his own hands. Surely his life appears to be located here. For as long as the flesh is alive, he lives. Therefore he sets his mind on the things of the " flesh " (Rom. 8:5) and is anxious about the things of the " world " (I Cor.

7:33; " world " here is equivalent to " flesh ") .

For mythical man the situation is somewhat different. In profound astonishment he knows about the mystery of the life he has in the flesh. To be sure, that life is perishable. But it is also inexhaustibly fertile. This mystery in which death and generation are inscrutably united he worships as he would worship gods. He serves the mystery in manifold ways in the cults of his gods. And so for the Christian faith " exchanging " the Creator for the creature is sin in its true sense. By it man forfeits his own salvation as well as the salvation of the world. The " exchange " may appear in the form of a cult, as for example in the worship of Baal, against which the Old Testament prophets battled incessantly. Or it may appear in the scrupulous observance of the stipulations of the law, by which the Jews of the later, postexilic time sought to preserve their religious world and win that " favor " before God and man which was so necessary to well-being in the Jewish world.

Something further must be said, however, about " exchanging the Creator for the creature " and the consequent " perversion " of the world from God's creation into a world of " nothingness." It must be made quite clear as to just what occurs, and that how, having occurred, it cannot be undone by man. So it is necessary to deal with what Paul called " the law of sin and death." The Biblical writers never speak of things in themselves. They refer to things as they are in man's relation to them. That peculiarity of the Biblical writers is nowhere clearer than in the concept of law as it appears in Paul's theology. He speaks, for example in Rom. 8:2 f., of the " law of sin and death," placing it in abrupt contrast to " the law of the Spirit of life." The obvious explanation might seem to lie in a dualistic world view having two laws. That is not the case, however. Rather, it is clear that in this passage Paul is speaking of two forms of one and the same law. He calls one form the law of death and the other the law of life.

The law of life has been changed into the law of death because the law has been "weakened by the flesh."

The meaning here is clear if one remembers the original sense of "law," found in the Old Testament saying, "Whoever keeps the law shall live" (Lev. 18:5). Here the law is the eternal will of God. Man stands under it in everything he is and does. The law in this sense directs man to God as to his lord, from whom he has being and life. He not only owes "this and that" to God, but in "this and that" he is indebted to God for himself. Therefore the law had to do originally with life. But man now observes that he lives on borrowed time. He falls into anxiety over life as he "has" it in the flesh. So he snatches at the law, which promises him life if he obeys it. The law in its original sense, however, speaks of the life man receives from God. It tells man he must place his trust, not in the evanescent creature, but in the Creator, who reveals himself as Creator when, from his "eternal power and deity," he calls into being that which is not. But man is seduced by the "flesh." He is as immediately aware of its perishableness as he is of his being alive. Nevertheless, he turns to this memory of the law itself, to the knowledge that he who keeps the law shall live, instead of turning to the Creator of the law. Through the care and preservation of life in the "flesh" — in the time of myth this took place primarily through the cultic worship of fertility gods — he believes he might overcome the decay of the "flesh." But since the life of the "flesh" is inevitably fleeting, with no possibility of being otherwise, the law itself, because it serves the "flesh," falls under the sway of corruption and death. In this misdirection of the law toward the care of the "life of the flesh," away from God whom the law in its original sense recalls, the "exchange" of the Creator for the creature takes place. The law should serve life, for it comes originally from God, who makes the dead alive. Instead, it gives birth to "the law of sin and death." In the law as it has now developed, the fear of death dominates man. In the rule of the fear of death sin also dominates man, the sin of exchanging the Creator for the creature.

To describe the law as it has now developed, Paul says that it is weakened by the " flesh." It is " weakened " because, when it is understood from the standpoint of concern for the life of the " flesh," it can no longer give a clear and resolute knowledge of God and of the life that can be lived only from God and the power of his Godhead. If anything, it is this law, seen from the standpoint of anxiety about the " flesh," which obstructs a clear knowledge of God and keeps man from obtaining life. At the same time, the law through this same " weakening " has gained an invincible power over man, driving him ever anew into the sin of that " exchange " which he is never able to recognize as such as long as the law retains its power over him.

To grasp Paul's thought rightly, it is crucial to recognize that the concept of the " flesh " is neither mythical nor metaphysical for him. For example, it is not a substance or a matter intrinsically opposed to God. Rather, it is historical. On the basis of the exegesis thus far adduced, we can say that by " flesh " he means the world and man in his relation to it in the most inclusive sense. It covers the kind of relation Paul describes when he says he is of the people of Israel " according to the flesh." This relation to the world is the kind that is possible because of the natural-historical order of the world and man's life in it. But the concept of " flesh " also includes the world and man in his relation to it as they have both developed through man's putting his trust in the creature — that is, in the world — rather than in the Creator. That means man has put his trust in the law that safeguards the life of the " flesh." In this relation both the world and man have undergone a profound and fateful transformation, a perversion of their original being into its opposite.

This perversion of the being of the world, brought about

through man's sin, is what Paul expresses by means of the concepts of " nothingness " and " decay " (Rom. 8:20 f.). The usual interpretation to the effect that these terms mean something like " destruction, conflict, suffering," which is " creation's portion," seems to me to miss the crucial point. It does not explain why the " eager longing of creation," which is subjected to " nothingness " and " decay," is directed toward the revealing of the " sons " of God and their liberty. Nor does it explain why creation awaits God's deliverance from this bondage, to which it is subjected " not of its own will but by the will of him who subjected it " (ch. 19 f.). This is only intelligible, if I may say so, if " nothingness " is not understood simply as the natural and therefore immediately known " transitoriness " of all earthly things. " Nothingness " must be seen as the nullifying power that gains dominion over the world and everything in it as well as over man. It gains that dominion when the law is weakened by the flesh and is thus changed from the law of the " life-giving Spirit " into the law of " sin and death."

The nature and power of this nothingness can be fully grasped only when one understands its effect. The call of God, which calls into being that which is not, is perverted into its opposite. Thereafter, everything that is, is called into nothingness. This is what is brought about because the law through the exchange of the Creator for the creature has become the law of " sin and death." In other words, it has become the law that serves sin and death in order to maintain its power over creation. For when man exchanges the Creator for the creature, when he impoverishes the creature and deprives him of his creaturely relation to God, he forfeits everything to which God's call has summoned him. Man's concern for the things of this world is then ruled necessarily by the nonbeing of the creature who has been deprived of his Creator. His anxiety draws him deeper and deeper into the " nothingness " of a fruitless and illusory service of the law. Vain and senseless indeed is this service of the law, for in serving it, man fancies himself to be serving God and winning life. In reality, however, he is denying God and entangling himself increasingly in death and its power over him. The " nothingness " and " decay " into which the world has fallen through man's sin, therefore, endure. They endure because by the power of the law that has become the law of " sin and death," the world holds man fast in the nothingness and decay of the service of the law.

When the nothingness of the world is understood in this sense, it is clear that the negative statements about the world that abound in the Bible cannot be the basis for a cosmological dualism such as dominates Hellenistic Gnosticism. According to Gnosticism, there are two worlds. One is a material-sensual world ruled by the " flesh " and therefore opposed and hostile to God. The other is a world ruled and sustained by the " Spirit " and so by God himself. In Gnosticism, " flesh " and " Spirit " are thought to be metaphysical and substantial dimensions, and so are accordingly the worlds that are determined by these dimensions. We have seen that for the Christian faith, which thinks historically rather than metaphysically, the " flesh " is not sinful in itself. All that is sinful is the exchange in which man puts his trust in the " flesh " and the life available to it, and in which he worships the creature instead of the Creator, thereby depriving God of the honor due him. Through such an exchange the one world that is God's creation is subjected to " nothingness." It is not a matter here of two worlds. But neither is it a matter of two laws. One law has been perverted through this very exchange from the law of the " life-giving Spirit " into the law of " sin and death."

In sharp contrast to Gnostic thought, therefore, the relation of man to the world is historical. It is a relation assigned to man's responsibility. But man has forfeited this responsibility through his trust in the " flesh." In this trust he has made the world his god: the world that God has given him as his son, the world of which it can be said that man is in but not of. Through his reliance on it, he has made the world something out of which he lives and on which he must trust with his whole being. One cannot be responsible *for* that on which he relies with his whole life, for he has become responsible *to* it. The lordship of man's former state has become bondage in his present state. Such bondage is forfeited lordship. Thus it is that responsibility to the world and to its law, the law " weakened by the flesh," is the forfeited responsibility *for* the world. It is impossible to exempt from the demands of honor a man who is dishonorable. In the same way, man is bound by responsibility for the world given him as son, as inheritance from God, if he has forfeited the responsibility. Even more, the responsibility adheres to him inextricably as a forfeiture in his entire being.

Now it becomes intelligible how Paul can say that the " expectant yearning of creation " itself awaits the manifestation and freedom of the sons of God. The " sons of God " are the men who can be manifested if God again bestows freedom on them. By " glorious freedom " he meant that this freedom is their glory open to the glory of God the Father and in this openness it participates anew in the " glory " of God. The whole eighth chapter of Romans speaks about receiving in faith the Son who is sent in the form of sinful flesh that this perverted freedom might be newly restored. And into this " freedom of the sons of God," the apostle Paul says, creation shall be delivered from the slavery of nothingness (Rom. 8:21), which is the negating power of the law.

The nothingness of the world to which the many negative statements of the Bible refer is not, therefore, the natural transitoriness of all things earthly. It is not even its supposed wickedness, from which only an ascetic disengagement could protect man. Nothing of that kind has even the least bit to do with the Christian faith — though it has been understood in this sense again and again.

This " nothingness " is, rather, the annihilating power of the law. By exchanging the Creator for the creature the law is perverted into the law of sin and death. By the authority of this law the world, deprived of its Creator, holds man fast in its bondage and worship. Man must be delivered from the law of the world if he is to be redeemed from the worship of the world and if the world is once again to be revealed as God's creation and as the divine inheritance vested with man.

8. FREEDOM FROM THE LAW

The nature of Christian freedom from the law can best be clarified by considering the powerful statement by the apostle Paul in Rom. 8:38. When Paul refers there to freedom and its foundation, he concludes with the confession, " I am sure that neither death, nor life, nor angels, nor principalities, nor things present, nor things to come, nor powers, nor height, nor depth, nor anything else in all creation, will be able to separate us from the love of God in Christ Jesus our Lord." Prior to this he spoke of man's freedom before God as son. Man's freedom from the law is grounded in this freedom. For the law that cannot separate the believer from the love of God is the law that rules the man who trusts in the world and in the powers of the world that he religiously worships. These powers are death and life, as they are understood within the limits of the world. They are the angels and principalities and powers, probably the power of the stars, that rule over present and future in the heights and the depths of the world.

To understand Paul's statement about the law, two things must be considered. First is the close and indissoluble connection linking the concept of law with the concept of the world. And second is the twofold sense in which Paul almost always speaks about the law. First, if one considers the close connection of the law with the world, one recognizes that whenever Paul speaks of the freedom from the law, he means by the concept of law pre-Christian piety — the piety of the Gentiles as well as of the Jews. In this piety, both Jews and Greeks are under sin and in the same way (Rom. 3:9). Secondly, one must understand in this context the twofold sense in which Paul speaks of the law. On the one hand, the law appears in the cultic ritual and moral commandments as they are met by man in the world and in the order of the world. These demands were given to the Jews in the law of the Old Testament. But this does not mean that they were withheld from the people who do not have the law, for the Gentiles show that the law is written on their hearts. What the law demands, they fulfill by nature (ch. 2:14 f.). On the other hand, Paul understands the law as the eternal will of God to which man is subject in everything that he is and does. The law, understood in this sense, directs man to God as his Lord, as we have seen. To this Lord he owes not simply "this or that," but, in "this or that," he owes himself. In the piety, however, in which man was imprisoned "before faith came" (Gal. 3:23; cf. ch. 4:1), the law directed man to the creature instead of to the Creator, to the world, to existence as man believed he must live it out of the world and its eternal order. And this very law which directed man to the world and its order was the law that held man captive in this piety. Everything he did was done because of the demands of the law understood in this way. But, seen from the Christian faith, the driving power of this piety was original sin, which had overcome man by virtue of this piety. The freedom from the law given man by the gospel of Jesus Christ is the freedom from the religious worship of the world and its powers. This freedom has its basis in the love of God, which, as the apostle Paul says, is in Christ Jesus, our Lord. For God gives us the spirit of sonship by him, the first born of the sons to whom he has predestined us to be equal as brothers. This spirit of sonship is the freedom in which man is able to live as son before God as father, watching over God's creatorhood and fatherhood in the world that is the inheritance vested with him. Freedom from the law is grounded in this freedom of the son for God. Freedom from the law is the freedom from the religious worship of the world. This negative sense of the freedom from the law as the deliverance from the religious worship of the world is important. It must not be overlooked, however, that this freedom also has a thoroughly positive sense. It could not be otherwise unless, as was true in Hellenistic Gnosticism, the world and the law belonging to it were intrinsically opposed and hostile to the reality of God. For the Christian faith, however, the world and the law are not intrinsically against God. In so far as they are against God, they are so only because of man, through the use he makes of them in worshiping them. Luther ventures to say that without man there would be no vanity and no "nothingness." For everything God has created was good and remains good (Gen. 1:31). It becomes bad and pernicious externally through no fault of its own but through the fault of man. For man, by his erring estimate or affection or misuse of the world, esteemed the world more highly than it really deserved. (W.A. 56, 372.)

We have already said that the "law" and the world are most closely bound up together. At least as long as it is in force, "law" always means the very being of the world that constitutes and orders it. Otherwise, law is nothing but an impotent literary document. If one has the idea of a world, a law ruling in it is always imagined. The meaning of " law " changes with the changes in the use one makes of the world. Hence, it is understandable that Paul, who, as no one else, had contemplated the significance of the " law " for the Christian faith, speaks about it with seemingly the sharpest contradictions. He can say that the " law " is the cause of sin and that it makes the sin exceedingly sinful. (Rom., ch. 7.) Everything depends on our having nothing to do with the law. Indeed, this is so radically true that we must die to that which keeps us captive. Then he poses the frightened question as to whether the " law " is sinful, and affirms that it is holy, right, and good. Yet he can also say that " all who rely on the works of the law " (literally, " who exist by works of the law ") " are under a curse," and that " no man is justified before God by the law " (Gal. 3:10 f.) . That appears again to be contradicted most sharply by the assertion that it is " the doers of the law who will be justified " (Rom. 2:13) .

In order to resolve these contradictions it is not enough to point to the double meaning the law had in Paul, of which we have already spoken. Consequently it is not the case that the negative statements of the " law " are valid for the law only in so far as it meets man in the world. Nor is it the case that the positive statements of the " law " are valid for the law only in so far as it is the eternal will of God. Rather, all the statements are valid with all their contradictions, here as well as there. A solution is possible only in the freedom for God which comes to us in faith and can be assured only by that faith. Moreover, freedom for God is so closely bound up with the man who is come of age as heir of the world that the one freedom is not possible without the other. Man could not be what God has created him, namely, one who should live in His presence in the freedom of sonship, if the world were not left to him as the responsible heir. Just as little, however, could he have this lordly freedom toward the world as an inheritance without the freedom for God.

Man's freedom toward the world is also two-sided. The double meaning is of crucial significance for our considerations. On the one hand, this is the freedom in which man cares for the world as the inheritance God vests with him. We have already spoken about that and have seen that such a freedom is possible only in faith. For man may be son and heir only by the power of God's fatherhood. The world, moreover, may be the creation of God only by God's creatorhood. Only as such can it be the whole, healthy world God has given man as his heir in which to live as a son. Faith alone can be aware of both God's fatherhood and his creatorhood. We also saw that this freedom toward the world, possible only in faith, in which man as son administers it as the inheritance bestowed by God, is the sole possible justification of human existence before God. For only with this freedom does man respond to God as God has created him. This, then, is the freedom by which the " law " is fulfilled as the eternal will of God.

Now, however, the inheritance is more than merely a possession. Nevertheless, it is always also a possession that the heir as its possessor has to administer by his own discretion. Freedom in the sense in which we have just spoken of it concerns the world as whole and healthy, which it is as God's creation. Freedom in the sense in which we have yet to discuss it concerns the world as it encounters man in " this and that." Here it is a matter of what Paul calls " works " (Rom. 2:6), of what man " has done in the body," or, as the passage in question can best be translated, it is a matter of " his own deeds " (II Cor. 5:10). Those are the works, or deeds, to whose proof and discrimination Paul summons his readers to determine whether they be " good or evil," whether they express " the good, acceptable, and perfect " will of God, whether, as Paul also says, they may be " what is excellent " (Rom. 2:18; Phil. 1:10). Of all these works it is said that the Christian should " test everything; hold fast what is good, abstain from every form of evil " (I Thess. 5:21-22).

What does it mean that the apostle expects of his readers such testing and discrimination of what they do or leave undone? This becomes obvious if one considers that for the Jews this demand refers primarily to the law of the Old Testament. According to the Jewish view, these commandments are to be observed word for word. Paul, himself facing the traditional law most passionately, exercises the criterion, " what is excellent," in his struggle against the Jewish legal piety. And for that reason he expects the members of the Galatian congregation to distinguish between valid and invalid in discussion with the Jewish-Christian agitators who made the fulfilling of the Jewish law the condition for membership in the Christian congregation. The presupposition for that critical attitude demanded toward the law is the knowledge granted with the freedom referred to earlier, to the effect that righteousness before God is only possible in faith.

For one who has this knowledge, the law is no longer what it was for Jewish legal piety. It is no longer the way that leads to the salvation of man and the world. In the pre-Christian relation of man to the world, the law was master of man. Now man has become master of the law. That does not mean he could treat the law arbitrarily. It means he can and will prove what is binding for him in the traditional law. Paul gives the criterion by which such a test shall be made. It is the commandment of love in which the whole law is concentrated. For " love does no wrong to a neighbor." (Rom. 13:10; compare Gal. 5:14.) Governed by this criterion, one will think about " whatever is true, honorable, just, pure, lovely, and gracious, if there is any virtue, anything worthy of praise " (Phil. 4:8). The most remarkable thing about this list is that the apostle " obviously uses concepts of popular moral philosophy " in order to express his meaning as to what is obligatory and valid for the Christian in the law. What corresponds to the will of God as he encounters man in the law is "the good, acceptable, and perfect" and that is not a particularly Christian criterion of action. The same act is proper to men in civic life. (Martin Dibelius, *Handbuch zum Neuen Testament,* Vol. 11, 3d edition, p. 95.) It is what Paul assumes man can know with the help of his reason.

The kind of freedom we have just referred to differs from the freedom in which man administers the world as his divine inheritance, as God's creation. The difference is that it cannot be said of this freedom that it is possible only in faith. On the contrary, man has to carry it out by his works and deeds and he has to be watchful of it by tests and criteria of the works demanded of him. Thus man's reason is called upon for this freedom and for the works demanded in it. These works are by no means meaningless. The evidence of that is that it is the reason which decides what shall be done or left undone. The paramount evidence, however, is that these works happen in and to the world that faith has known as God's creation. Without prejudice to man's reasonable decision concerning them, they are subject to judgment and reward on God's part. Everyone has to account for his works "before the judgment seat of Christ" and "receive good or evil, according to what he has done in the body" (II Cor. 5:10).

What is the relation between the apostle's doctrine of justification by faith alone and these recurrent statements that deal with divine rewards for works? (Rom. 2:6; 14:10; I Cor. 3:13 ff.; 4:5; 11:32.) To answer that question, two things must be observed. One is that the reward for works must not be understood as justification in the proper sense, which is an ultimate decision about man. On the occasion of the controversy over factions in the Corinthian congregation, Paul says of the teachers of the gospel that their work of preaching will be tried in the fire of the Judgment Day and they will receive punishment or reward on that basis. Their work is the human, individual method of their preaching. One could even say it is the teaching or the theology unique to each teacher, with which he seeks to make the gospel accessible to his hearers. In distinction to the foundation for preaching laid once for all, which is Christ, Paul calls these the " building " made from " gold, silver, precious stones, wood, hay, stubble," according to the individual peculiarity of the teacher. The condition of this building will be revealed by fire, and the teacher will receive a reward or suffer loss, depending on the way it stands the test. However, he himself will be saved, but only as one who has gone through fire. (I Cor. 3:13 ff. and also ch. 11:32.)

There is a second thing that must be observed regarding these Pauline expressions about reward for works. It is a presupposition entirely self-evident for Paul that the works in question here have not been done with a view toward justification before God. Rather, they have been submitted to the decision of God in expectation of the Last Judgment. Hence, in the passage just quoted concerning the work of the teacher of the gospel, Paul says of himself, when attacked because of his preaching, that he was not aware of any offense of which he is guilty. But judgment of his preaching by his opponents does not disturb him. Even less does he rely on the good conscience he has concerning his preaching. For beyond these he submits himself to the judgment of the Lord, " who will bring to light the things now hidden in darkness and will disclose the purposes of the heart. Then every man will receive his commendation from God." (Ch. 4:1 ff.)

9. THE TWOFOLD FREEDOM

We have seen how two meanings of man's freedom in his relation to the world can be distinguished. On the one hand, there is freedom as it is possible only in faith, and on the other hand, there is freedom as it concerns the action and the works of man. If one observes this distinction, one can understand why Paul makes contradictory assertions about one and the same law, claiming that it causes man life as well as death. We have already shown that Paul knows two forms of the law. One is the form in which it meets man in the world and its order, demanding works from him. The other is the form in which it meets him as the eternal will of God, demanding the man himself. And those contradictory statements are meant so that each of them pertains to both forms of the law. We have seen that the law, in the form in which it meets man as the eternal will of God, can be fulfilled only in faith. For the man himself as he is here demanded is the man as he lives in the freedom for God, which he can appropriate for himself only as that which God bestows on him. Understood in this way, it is the law that turns out to be life to man. Works are no help in obtaining this freedom and fulfilling the eternal will of God by it. On the contrary, the mere intention of fulfilling the will of God by works rather than by faith already means that one denies himself to God and his will. Hence, Paul does not only say nobody can be justified by works (Gal. 2:16; Rom. 3:20, 28; 4:5; 11:6). He ventures the much sharper formulation that "all who rely on the works of the law," that is, who intend to be justified by the works of the law, "are under a curse" (Gal. 3:10; cf. II Cor. 3:6 ff.; Rom. 7:8; 8:2). The "works" referred to here are those which man does with the intent of becoming justified before God in compliance with the law as it meets him in the world, be it a cultic-religious or a moral law.

This intention maintains itself by relying upon its own achievements. Paul calls it " boasting " and " confidence in the flesh " (II Cor. 11:18 and Phil. 3:4). This intention constitutes the law as the law that brings man under a curse and kills him, because it is not fulfilled in this way. For it wishes to achieve by works what only faith can do, namely, the fulfillment of the eternal will of God. If the law, in the form in which it meets man in the world and in its order, remains limited to something to be done in the world, it has a good sense in this limitation and man is able to fulfill it. But the intention to achieve righteousness before God takes away this good meaning and gives the law a goal that lies beyond all human possibilities. For if man tries to fulfill the law by his works, it can only mean that he puts his own work in the place of God's grace. But then " grace would no longer be grace " (Rom. 11:6). God's " foolishness " would be supplanted by the wisdom of man, God's " weakness " by the power of man (I Cor. 1:21 ff.), and God's glory would be changed into man's boasting. Consequently, man is given the " spirit of stupor, eyes that should not see and ears that should not hear " (Rom. 11:8), which is what God gave the Jews who could not bear the brightness of the glory of God on the face of Moses (II Cor. 3:7). Man " stands," then, no longer in freedom (Gal. 5:1). The law as God's eternal will calling him into freedom and faith and in this way into life now proves to be death to him (Rom. 7:10). Faith has become empty because it has not taken care of what was entrusted to it.

Due to this risk, again and again in the New Testament there are warnings to be awake and to be free of the world. It is a fateful mistake if these warnings are understood in an ascetic or moral sense. Such a misunderstanding is perennial, and it is virtually unavoidable if the freedom for God is not conceived in the clear meaning in which the apostle Paul has understood it and proclaimed it as the core of the gospel in his doctrine of justification by faith alone. The clear knowledge of the freedom for God made accessible by the Christian faith must therefore remain lost if the moral or ascetic misunderstanding of those warnings is not clearly recognized. These warnings must be understood against the background of what Paul has conceived as the real sin of man. That sin is the exchange of the Creator for the creature. Therewith man exchanges "the glory of the immortal God for images resembling mortal man or birds or animals or reptiles." And man does it, so Paul says (Rom. 1:22 f.), "claiming to be wise." What Paul means in speaking about God's "glory" is the power that is God's deity and that calls into being what is not, "from whom and through whom and to whom are all things." Paul here calls God immortal. He does not simply say that God is immortal in and for himself, but that he is the One from whom all life inexhaustibly proceeds. Now, if Paul says that man supplants this glory and what is given with it by an image resembling mortal man or birds, or animals, or reptiles, and if he says, moreover, that man does it "claiming to be wise," it seems clear to me that by this image Paul has the idea of something that seems divine in the fact of the wisdom man has through his intercourse with the world. Therefore, one rightly understands these warnings about becoming free of the world only if one conceives that they intend for faith to insist upon the distinction between the two forms of the law and in this way to safeguard the freedom for God as the sole possible justification of man before God.

For another reason, this warning is even more urgent. As we have seen even of the law as it encounters man in the world and in its order, demanding works of him, it is true that the law is "holy and just and good" (ch. 7:12; compare ch. 13:1 ff.). Nothing, therefore, could be farther from the truth than to think that by his doctrine of justification by faith alone Paul has warned against works or has detracted from their positive meaning. That could not possibly be his meaning as long as man lives in the world and therefore cannot be without works. As Paul understands faith, it has its proper place precisely in the doing of works. Not, of course, in the sense that faith is some sort of "motive power" for works. Rather, faith has its proper place in works in the sense that man needs faith in order not to come under the rule of the law by trusting in his works and thus bringing the curse upon himself. If the works the law demands from man as it meets him within the world are done without faith, man continually stands in danger. He may exchange his own righteousness for the righteousness valid before God, which is righteousness by grace alone. If he does so, his righteousness can be no other than what he has acquired by his works in the world and without which he would even lose his right to existence in the world. But here is the basis of the calamity that now must follow. What concerns this man is not only righteousness as the world values it, which is nothing but the world. Rather, he seeks the righteousness of God as Paul indicates the Jews did. But what he does "is not enlightened" (ch. 10:2). That means that he acts without faith and thinks that the righteousness acquired in and before the world is the righteousness of God. By this confusion he has brought about an exchange of the Creator with the creature, which is sin properly conceived. In the stupor of man's spirit (ch. 11:8) brought about by the exchange, this righteousness has become the object of man's zeal. It is the righteousness of a religiously worshiped world. What pertains to the deepest darkness to which the human spirit can fall can now be said of this man. The good that he wants he does not do, but the evil he does not want is what he does (ch. 7:19). That good which he wants but does not do is the righteousness of God. The evil that he does not want but does is that which he offers to the creature, to the world — the worship and service that belong to the Creator. He must do it, because he stands under the power of that exchange authorized by the "law." That is what Paul means when he adds this next verse: "Now if I do what I do not want, it is no longer I that do it, but sin which dwells within me." This sin is the religious worship of the world and its law.

With the power of fate this calamitous trap holds prisoner those fallen into it. The trap is the calamity from which faith frees man. But faith can do it only by fulfilling its most proper task. That task involves defending the freedom of man for God where it is continuously and, at the same time, most profoundly threatened. That is the place where the law with its demands encounters man in the world and its order. Out of the freedom for God protected by it, faith may divest the law, in the form in which it encounters man here, of its religious or demonic power and so surrender to the reason of man. That is what Paul indicates with the exceptionally keen statement: "All things are permitted me, but not all things are expedient." (I Cor. 6:12; 10:23.) It is obvious that this statement does not speak in favor of the "enlightenment" as it was already known in late antiquity. It is much more a word of faith.

The occasion for this sentence was a discussion that originated in the Corinthian congregation. The discussion had to do with whether a Christian was permitted to eat food offered to idols (I Cor. 8:1 ff. and ch. 10:14 ff.). The food referred to is the flesh of sacrificial beasts that was not burned on the altar but brought to the market for sale. Some members had misgivings about eating such food because it made them appear to be participating in the pagan worship. For according to the ancient view, the essence of the gods to whom the sacrifice is offered is present in such flesh through the very performance of the sacrifice. Paul proceeds on the basis of his decision that these gods, if they exist — and he is of the opinion that they do — still have no power over those who believe on the one God, the Father, of whom are all things, and we in him, and on the one Lord Jesus Christ, by whom are all things, and we by him. But some lacked this knowledge, and because their thinking was not free from the association with the gods, they would eat the flesh not as ordinary flesh but as sacrificial flesh. By virtue of their lack of knowledge, their weak conscience would be offended. But now, the apostle continues, meat does not commend us to God. If we eat it, we are none the better; if we do not eat it, we are none the worse. Before God only one thing is decisive. Whatever we do, whether we eat or drink or whatever else, we must do it to the glory of God. According to the immediate context, to do something to God's glory is to do it with thanksgiving (I Cor. 10:30). This thankfulness pertains not simply to the object of the deed in question, such as the flesh that is eaten in the passage referred to. The object of this thankfulness is, rather, that the entire existence of man is justified by faith. To do something with thanks, therefore, means to do it in the faith that alone justifies man. If the deed is done in faith, before God there is no difference between the deed of the one who eats flesh and the deed of the one who abstains. He " who eats, eats in honor of the Lord, since he gives thanks to God; while he who abstains, abstains in honor of the Lord and gives thanks to God " (Rom. 14:6). The concern here is not the doing of this or that, but the entire existence of man justified by faith. The sentences immediately following show that: " None of us lives to himself, and none of us dies to himself. If we live, we live to the Lord, and if we die, we die to the Lord; so then, whether we live or whether we die, we are the Lord's. For to this end Christ died and lived again, that he might be Lord both of the dead and of the living." But what a man does in faith, whether he eat or not, he must himself decide in the light of the circumstances. This freedom is given him by faith. By it he knows it is not what he does that justifies him before God but only the faith in which he does it.

This, then, is what is meant by the sentence, " All things are permitted me, but not all things are expedient." One understands this sentence in its full significance only if one comprehends that by this very means faith fulfills its most proper task of safeguarding the freedom for God. Faith is able to fulfill its task only by giving man and his reason the freedom to decide what he shall do. This freedom of decision is not simply granted as a sort of permission. Faith must insist on it, for only in this way is it able to fulfill its task. We have already seen that man can " appropriate " the freedom entrusted to him by God only if he has his own world to which he is independently related in the possibility of free decision. Therefore, faith is able to accomplish the task to be fulfilled by it in this one way. Safeguarding the freedom vested with man by God, faith must make man's independence of the world available to him. In this way faith saves the world from becoming the object of religious worship. And it saves the law, as it meets man in the world, from the same religious worship. These are most closely connected. Only when faith fulfills this task, which means only when it is justifying faith in the rigorously Pauline and Reformation sense herein developed, has it the power and courage for this deliverance. On the other hand, faith is able to keep the freedom for God pure and develop its sole justifying power only if it ends all religious worship of the law and in this way surrenders to the reason.

Only under these conditions is that complete understanding of self-consciousness possible which originates in the reflection of faith calling man to himself and to his

" coming of age." This self-consciousness is a twofold thing in the way it expresses the double meaning of " coming of age." In the presence of God it is one thing. In relation to the world it is another. The freedom contained in this " coming of age " we call in each case " the freedom of the son," in order to express the unity of these two kinds of self-consciousness. One and the same son is conscious of his sonship in two ways. He knows that as the son he is nothing of himself. He is what he is only in virtue of his father and of what he receives from him. This is meant not simply in the sense that once upon a time in the past he was begotten of his father and received his sonship. If that were all he had, he would really never have known his father as a father or himself as a son. Rather, he knows himself as one who is receiving his sonship from the constancy of the father's fatherhood. He knows that he remains in this position only when he gives himself to the father in the same constancy of sonship. At the same time, he has this knowledge about himself in the fact that he administers the inheritance vested with him by his father in the independence of one " come of age." Both taken together constitute sonship and are indissolubly bound up together, just as they are contained in faith and safeguarded by it.

As for the freedom and independence of man in his relation to the world, they are made accessible by faith in virtue of the freedom of God that faith preserves. That this independence is subsequently maintained and responded to is an autonomous achievement of the reason. In the same way, it is an understanding of the world and its laws that is no longer hindered by the religious worship of the world. Indeed, by reserving all worship exclusively for God, the Christian faith removed the hindrances that had rendered man's independent relation to the world impossible. But, if I may say so, that this independence was set in process and elaborated could be accomplished only by man's reason. Actually, it did not take place for fifteen centuries.

The primary reason for that is that for the Christian faith the matter of paramount importance was the deliverance of man from the world and the power of its law, in keeping with its most proper task of safeguarding the freedom for God. The second reason can be found in the character of medieval thought, which had never liberated itself from classical thought. For one thing, it was not able to think the freedom of the Christian faith resolutely enough to enable man to encounter God without the mediation of institutions of a worldly kind. Nor was it capable of an elaboration of the independence of man toward the world. For upon the medieval man the religious worship of the world obtrudes again and again from classical thought as well as from the views of pagan nations converted to the Christian faith. The medieval man was content to convert this alien worship to Christianity only to a limited extent. Under these circumstances, it could hardly fail that the understanding of faith and its justifying power worked out by Paul in his discussion with the Jewish religion of law was considerably obscured.

One ought to be cautious, then, in adducing the reasons for the breakdown of the medieval world. It is not because the Middle Ages were unable to think about the Christian faith and the freedom for God that faith protects and that surrenders the world to man for his independent administration. And it is not because the church understood the faith in such a way that it based a world upon it that it thereupon prosecuted as the attorney for this faith. It is because this faith was not at all qualified to provide the foundation for a structure in the world such as the medieval church was erecting. Some deeper reflection upon the faith on which its essence turns, even if only by presentiment, must account for the shaking of the structure of this world in its whole artful coherence. In these perpetual tensions and contradictions the medieval world finally broke down. Through these tensions, the authority and power by which the church ruled the world and attempted to hold it in order became more and more questionable.

10. THE ORIGIN OF SUBJECTIVISM

Two spiritual forces developed on the ruins of the medieval world. Taken together, they constituted the sonship that the Christian faith had made accessible to man in his relation to God and the world. One force was the freedom for God; the other, the freedom toward the world. Each freedom had its own kind of human consciousness. The former was evident in Luther's Reformation; the latter, in what we could call modern science, or, more comprehensively, modern thought. Both these forces were originally connected, since in faith they expressed the mature sonship of man toward God and the world. Later, however, they were separated.

Man's freedom for God, which God granted man in Jesus Christ, was expressed by Luther in a purity and power rivaled before his time only by the apostle Paul. Luther was able to open up the whole of space to man's independence toward the world, an independence that was man's through the freedom of faith. It might be said that in this regard Luther went even beyond Paul, if not in principle at least in the particular and explicit handling of problems. The cardinal instance is the extraordinarily important problem of ethics. In his doctrine of the two kingdoms, " the Kingdom of Christ " and " the kingdom of the world," as he called them, Luther repudiated the medieval church's claim to sovereignty over the world and its orders, a claim made in the name of faith. The church could make such a claim only unlawfully. It could do so only by making a law out of the gospel of man's free sonship before God, which is precisely what it did. That is why it can be said that Luther granted autonomy to man's life in the world and to the orders of life. This worldly life, so he says, is " subjected and entrusted to the reason because the worldly government should adjudicate not the salvation of the soul and the eternal good, but only bodily and temporal goods which God subordinates to man " (W.A. 51, 242). Luther is himself aware that in liberating the " worldly professions " from the tutelage of the church he has done something great and decisive. As he once confessed, " since apostolic times there has been no doctor nor author, no theologian nor jurist, who has so gloriously and clearly confirmed, instructed, and comforted the conscience as I have done, although of course through the grace of God, as I full well know " (W.A. 38, 102 f.).

Luther had hardly any contact with the modern scientific knowledge of the world that was developing in his time. It would have been strange to him. From the standpoint of knowledge of the world or world view, he belonged entirely to the Middle Ages. In an occasional comment about Copernicus he reveals the distrustful reserve of the conservative. He was a conservative in every concern that did not directly involve faith. The actual attitude of the University of Wittenberg to a young professor, Rhaeticus, however, is revealing. Rhaeticus was personally related to Copernicus and endorsed his doctrine. Nevertheless, by his attitude toward Rhaeticus, Luther acknowledged the autonomy that belonged to science. It belonged to science in the same way that it belonged to the practical life in the world, through the freedom of faith. As Werner Elert says, " The church's limitation of itself to preaching the gospel in Luther's sense necessarily expressed itself in Lutheran circles in complete freedom of research and instruction in the natural sciences." That situation first changed when in the Evangelical churches the Bible was used as a lawbook of faith, and hence as a canon for natural science, just as it had always been in the medieval church. (Compare Werner Elert, *Morphologie des Luthertums,* Vol. 1, München, 1931, pp. 363 ff.) Thereby, however, Luther's understanding of faith as that which alone justifies was lost.

Indeed, Luther's successors attempted to conserve the understanding of faith that he brought to light. But due to the religio-political situation of the time they became involved in confessional struggles and turned the "article on justification" into simply one theological "article" among others "on" which one must believe as he believes "on" the others. Theological thought turned again into a scholastic formalism from which Luther had liberated it. As a result, the one great theme of man's freedom for God and of man's consequent freedom toward the world no longer prevailed as it did in the thought of Luther. The question of the confessional correctness of individual theological "articles" prevailed instead. Likewise, the force was lost from the bold conclusions for the relation of the Christian to the world, which Luther had drawn as an implication of his understanding of the faith. It was now necessary to struggle in the name of the faith and in its defense against reason's working out man's relation to the world autonomously. Thus it came about that the Bible which Luther learned to read exclusively as the book of faith and taught others to read in the same way again became the lawbook of the world.

This development held most important consequences for the discussion of man's independence toward the world as it was achievable by the reason. It started when the end of the medieval world increasingly broke down the church's hitherto undisputed sovereignty over the spiritual life. As we have already said, Luther had imposed no alien law either on the life of the world or on its new science (in so far as science entered into his consideration). He achieved this attitude by the power of the justifying faith and man's freedom for God, which it conserved. For the liberation of the world and its laws as the Christian faith achieves it corresponds to its proper task in the most precise way. With an imperturbable clarity that resisted all the attempts of this confused time to cloud it, Luther knew that the faith is able to remain justifying faith only when it carries out this liberation. This is the faith of which Luther said that it " holds sway over all that is and is not, both sin and virtue " (W.A. 7, 216). In this way, then, the distinction between both these forces remains legitimate, which, taken together, constitutes man's sonship toward God and the world accessible in the Christian faith. The distinction retained its original meaning — to liberate the world and its law from religious worship and to persevere in this liberation.

With such a distinction of the two forces, the freedom for God and the freedom toward the world, science was able to remain true to itself. The freeing of the world and its laws from religious worship corresponds to the most proper task of faith — to safeguard man's freedom for God. But in exactly the same way it expresses the nature of reason which proves itself by making man independent toward the world, keeping the work of science free from every religious worship of the world and its laws. For wherever science indulges in such worship, it abrogates its essential task. As scientific hypotheses for the clarification of particular facts, " God and the decrepit, half-religious concepts which one puts in his place in modern times signify but imperfect stages of science. With the progress of knowledge they find themselves in continual and seldom honorable retreat." (C. F. v. Weizsäcker, *Zum Weltbild der Physik,* 2d revised edition, 1944, p. 144.)

The relation between faith and science, however, became essentially different after Luther's death. Through the development that set in, faith increasingly lost its sole justifying power. Consequently, its unique task of defending man's freedom for God could no longer be fulfilled with the bold resoluteness made possible through the understanding that Luther discovered. It now became unavoidable that works, however interpreted, should receive justifying significance alongside faith as it was henceforth understood. But that had the consequence that man's independence toward the world must be limited at least to the extent that, alongside faith, legally demanded works were necessary for man's justification before God — works that were demanded by faith itself. Thus in the name of faith as understood at this time, man's independence toward the world had to be limited anew. And that means that it was necessary to impose laws upon science in the name of faith, laws to which faith itself submits when it lets its validity become dependent on certain works to be achieved.

Reaction from the side of science was inevitable. For scientific thought since the beginning of modern times had by nature the task of working out man's independence toward the world. Science can acknowledge no other law than the law of its methodical questioning, for which in principle there can exist no other limit than the one it postulates on the basis of its method. That certainly does not mean that scientific thought can get to the point where questions no longer exist. It simply means that each answer gives rise to a new question to which it seeks an answer in the same way it answered earlier questions. In the ensuing discussion with the faith of the church and its theology, science won the right to an autonomous responsibility for its activity, unlimited by such alien laws as the faith of the church posed for it. It thereafter occurred, as it often does with such reactions, that science succumbed to the same kind of necessity that dominated the faith of the church when the church found it necessary to limit the autonomy of science in the interests of what the church believed. This domination originated from the fact that the faith against its own nature was tempted anew to a religious worship of the world and its laws. From this worship it derived the right and the obligation to demand of science the fulfillment of the same laws. Science for its part appealed to the same argument in its defense, namely, that of religious worship.

Obviously, the religious worship to which science appealed in the face of the church's faith could not be the same as that which had tempted the faith and to which it succumbed. This religious worship, rather, claims the world and demands the subjection of man and his deeds to its law. Science, or reason, has the unalterable task of methodically achieving man's independence toward the world by the fulfillment of its own laws. But science would have to give up if it were to engage in such religious worship of the world and its laws. Yet science can direct its religious worship to whatever is its end and its task, namely, to man's independence toward the world. C. F. v. Weizsäcker has given an illustration of such religious worship in the " symbol " of the infinity of the world. He means that this symbol has supported the world view of modern science. (" Die Unendlichkeit der Welt. Eine Studie Über das Symbolische in der Naturwissenschaft," in the book *Zum Weltbild der Physik,* 2d edition, 1940, pp. 124 ff.) Nicholas of Cusa, who first taught the infinity of the world, understood it as a symbol for the infinity of God who " had shared with the world as much of his perfection as possible, even though it was still different from him " *(ibid.,* p. 137). Giordano Bruno, " the next great proponent of the infinite world, though he also made the distinction between God and the world conceptually, actually only spoke about the world. The brightness of infinity falls upon the world " *(ibid.,* p. 142). As B. Grothuysen says, in his *Phil-*

osophical Anthropology: " The man who speaks here in Giordano Bruno of his feelings toward the world is no longer man as the cosmic nature but the individual who brings to expression his reaction toward the world. The individual's experience of the world is no longer something worldly; it is something unique. It has the connotation not so much of the world as ultimately of the individual considering the world, of the self." Hence, this individual sees " in the infinite striving of his soul the equivalent of the infinity of the world " (*Handbuch der Philosophie,* Section III, p. 141) . This is what Weizsäcker means when he says that the infinity of the world is " the most obvious symbol of the faith in progress." With it as the " idea of an infinite field of activity," the " symbol of satisfaction " is given for the " life feeling of the modern man," for his infinite striving, which is deeply disturbed by " every thought of a boundary still so distant." When the new knowledge of today's physics rendered this image of the infinity of the world impossible, " at least one discomfort remained which was intensified in many cases to the point of a passionate contradiction " (*ibid.,* pp. 160 ff.) . This occurred, although one was convinced of the logical correctness of the knowledge that led to the suspension of this view of the infinity of the world.

In a word, religious worship is given to the human reason here, as it had begun to work itself out in modern science in completely autonomous responsibility for its own lawfulness, in man's independence toward the world. In worshiping man's reason, this independence takes on a meaning it did not originally have. By " originally " is meant the working out that is possible to science as such. In its original sense it can never be otherwise related than to the immediate data and what can be concluded with certainty from this data through demonstration. The independence of man toward the world, arrived at in this way, can always, therefore, be related only to individual data, never to the whole of existence. But religious worship enters as soon as this meaning, related to the whole, supports the independence of man, or, to say the same thing, as soon as it is understood in terms of world view. Then it is a matter of an attitude of man toward the world in which, as Heidegger says, he " can be the one being who gives all being its measure and applies the plumb line " (*Holzwege,* p. 87) .

Therewith arises " that kind of human being who occupies the sphere of human capacity as the space of measure and achievement for the mastering of being in its wholeness " (*ibid.,* p. 84) . Man now changes into " that being upon whom all being is grounded in the manner of its being and its truth. Man changes into the relating center of being itself " (*ibid.,* p. 81) . This prerogative as " a sub-ject (as ground to what lies on the ground) , distinguished by its being essentially unconditioned, originates from the claim of man to a *fundamentum absolutum inconcussum veritatis* (as a ground of truth in the sense of certainty, unshakable, resting upon itself) " (*ibid.,* p. 98) . Man derives this certainty from the certainty of the proposition " which asserts that simultaneous (at the same time and also continuously) with the thinking of man he is undoubtedly present with himself, that is now: given himself " (*ibid.,* p. 100) . The thinking of man receives the sense of " realize, a realizing relation to the realized " (*ibid.,* p. 100) . (" Realize " is a possible translation of Heidegger's *" vorstellen "* and bears the meaning of " conceive as reality, apprehend clearly," but not without the undertone of " make realistic, give apparent reality.") And being in its wholeness is understood by this thinking in such a way " that it is primarily and solely being in so far as it is posited through the realizing-producing man." [*" Vorstellend-herstellenden Menschen," ibid.,* p. 82. If one hears in the word " realize " the twofold sense of " conceive as reality " and " make realistic," he will have the best translation of *" den vorstellend-herstellenden Menschen."*] What, then, is the essence of the subjectivity of this subject, this "realizing-producing" essence into which man has here changed? The essence of subjectivity is "the unconditional unbaring of the sphere of possible objectivization and of the right to decision regarding this sphere" (*ibid.,* p. 101).

11. THE THEOLOGICAL DISCUSSION WITH SUBJECTIVISM

By subjectivism I mean man's independence toward the world when that independence is understood as a kind of world view. There is rather general conviction in theology today that this subjectivism is the reason for the assertion that faith is the presupposition of everything included in its world view. One gets the idea, therefore, that one could counter subjectivism only if one opposed to it some "objective basis for faith." For it is felt that only by some such "objective" reality of its subject could one protect faith from dissolving into a mere "attitude immanent to man" and keep the reality of faith from being vitiated. If the nature of this subjectivism is grasped, it is easy to see that such an attempt to guarantee the objective certainty of faith by some prior knowledge of it as an object is subjected to the ban of this subjectivistic thinking and by no means escapes it. For it is the nature of this thinking to objectify the being it thinks. It realizes (*vor-stellt*) what it thinks. That means it objectifies (*vergegenständlicht*) what it thinks.

The "modern freedom of subjectivity" is this independence of man toward the world. Modern science wrested from the church the independent responsibility for its action as its own right, a responsibility unrestricted by alien laws. To justify and guarantee the independence, science took its own philosophical foundation from modern subjectivism. The foundation in world view leads to the fullest absorption of "the modern freedom of subjectivity," that is, man's independence toward the world, as science now understands it, into "objectivity as it corresponds to subjectivity." This objectivity is the "fullest technical control over the world" (Heidegger, *op. cit.*, p. 103).

Theology may now attempt to protect its faith from modern subjectivism by asserting the "objectivity of its basis for faith," by claiming a "historical factuality" for its so-called facts of salvation. If it does, however, it does so under the compulsion of subjectivistic thinking itself. Indeed, in this way theology will regain for faith what science contested in it, namely, certainty as science defines it. Clearly, this can never be the certainty of a subject that, in the sense of modern subjectivism, is certain of itself. But neither can it be the certainty of an "objective" reality. Where one attempts such certainty he does so because, without knowing it, he thinks subjectivistically and succumbs to the ultimate consequence of this kind of thinking.

The theological discussion with subjectivism must enter at an earlier point. It must enter where subjectivism has its source. Man was enthroned as the subject who as "the foundation concentrates everything on himself" (*ibid.*, p. 81). This led to the situation in which science found it necessary to wrest its right to free research from the faith of the church, which had tried to prescribe its limits. Science then succumbed to the temptation to create a kind of world view identical with subjectivism. That is the way subjectivistic thought came to prevail. Theology, which has the responsibility for understanding the faith, has every ground, therefore, to begin its argument with subjectivism, where the proper cause of its origin is to be sought. If we are on the right track here, this cause must be sought with faith, or, more correctly, with that understanding of faith which occasioned science's yielding to the temptation to construct a world view. As we have already seen, that was a faith which was no longer understood in the rigorous sense of the apostle Paul and Luther as the faith that alone justifies. It was, therefore, no longer the faith whose most proper task was to watch over man's freedom for God. In the fulfillment of its task such a faith should be able to free the world and its law from every form of religious worship. In consequence of this liberation, it should be able to hand over to the reason as a trustee the task of working out man's independence toward the world and its laws.

The rise of subjectivism became possible or was at least essentially determined by the lack of such a faith. The most important matter in theology's discussion with modern subjectivism, therefore, is to regain the proper understanding of faith in the absence of which subjectivism arose. I say deliberately that this understanding of faith must be regained in the *discussion* with subjectivism. The domain of this kind of thinking is too comprehensive to withdraw from it without the profoundest reflection on its nature. One dare not bypass it. For as Heidegger characterized it, it belongs to the "genuinely essential forces of our age which work as they work untouched by any banal estimate" (*ibid.,* p. 89). It has filled our language with its meaning, affecting its concepts and words not only in individual instances but also as a whole. It provides the vocabulary under whose domain we are now obliged to think. Now an understanding of faith (note I say an *understanding* of faith, not the faith itself) is possible only by thinking it. Nothing is accomplished by obtaining one's understanding of faith from the warehouse stocked by the very theological tradition by which one tries to ward off subjectivism.

In trying to regain an understanding of faith through

the discussion with modern subjectivism, one does not quite expect what is unsuited to its nature and what subjugates it to an alien law. We have seen in Paul as well as in Luther that it is the most proper task of faith, even the most proper activity of its thought, to safeguard the freedom for God as it is newly regained for man through the death and resurrection of Jesus Christ, to deliver the world and its law from every kind of religious worship, and so enable man's independence toward the world and its law. Now the pagan-religious (or as we may better say, the mythical) worship of the world and its law is no longer the serious temptation for modern man that it was for the early Christian man. Even if one meant that something like a mythical feeling for life and a mythical aspect of the world is still the presupposition for artistic creation today, one could not say it. The world in which we live and in which we make our existential decisions is no longer the world surrounding men with mysterious eternal orders, to which it was man's highest wisdom and virtue to adapt himself obediently. Indeed, the powers of law hold sway; but they have ceased being divine. We have attained a knowledge of them, and by the help of that knowledge, power over them. The mere desire for such power would have seemed a sacrilege to antiquity and the Middle Ages. In place of divine powers there are now energies whose lawful activity man investigates with the help of modern science. On the basis of this research, man has laid well-calculated plans for taking these powers into his service.

This knowledge and authority has forced man into a responsibility both for the world and for its being and remaining a world. In the process the law of the world assumes an authority over man, although in quite a new way, that is not in the least inferior to the authority exercised by it in the time of the mythical-religious worship of the world. Signs of this power are pre-eminently the utopian and optimistic hopes for unlimited progress in the world.

These hopes, expressed today particularly in the form of political world views, bind men in a hardly less powerful way than religions had bound them in earlier days. Curiously enough, modern scientific thought, quite contrary to its proper nature, easily succumbs to the temptation to world view. The explanation for that must not be sought in the pride in knowledge attained and the power achieved by that knowledge. It must be found as well in the tremendous weight of responsibility increasingly burdening the modern man as a result of the extent of this knowledge and power over the world. To this responsibility is bound a dark anxiety. It is often only surmised. It seldom penetrates fully into consciousness, and therefore it is predictable only with great difficulty. The supposition is that there is an uncanny fate weighing heavily and capable of being exposed only with difficulty. But even if the fate is of a sort that can be exposed, it will not be uncovered so long as the thinking about it is dominated by subjectivism. For this very subjectivism, and the dominion it exercises over our thinking as one of the " uniquely essential forces of our time," is this fate. In subjectivism, this fate, the law of the world, has seized man anew.

Paul speaks of the same set of facts in Rom., ch. 7. The distinction is simply that in Paul's case we have the law in its *pre-Christian* form. He has introduced its fateful power in this chapter in Romans. The form in which the law seizes man in modern subjectivism is different. We could call it *post-Christian*. The law Paul refers to is, on the one hand, the law of the mythical powers of the world and of the eternal order of the cosmos, in so far as he is thinking of the pagan peoples. On the other hand, in so far as he is thinking of the Jews, it is the law of postexilic Judaism, a law to which deity was virtually attributed. In both cases the law is the order of the world, pre-existent and endowed with eternal validity. As Paul says, man was confined by this law until faith came — he was held in custody as an heir who is not yet of age. Even though he is lord of all, he is under tutors and governors, hence, indistinguishable from a slave (Gal. 3:23 and ch. 4:1 f.). Paul is able to expose the fate by whose power the law subjects the pre-Christian man. His ability to do so rests on his being able to see the coming revelation of faith (Gal. 3:22) as one who can "see foreseeing" (*vordenkend bedenken;* compare Heidegger, *op. cit.,* p. 103). He can see that being kept in custody is not the final possibility for the human being. The question remains whether subjectivism is the sort of fate that has overcome man and that can be overcome only by being uncovered. If it is, then it is most important whether we succeed in revealing that the law that seizes man and his world in subjectivism is a law that keeps modern man confined to its custody in the same way in which the law Paul speaks about did to the pre-Christian man.

12. THE POST–CHRISTIAN FORM OF THE LAW

The form in which the law has established itself over modern thought by the power of subjectivism is determined by the Christian faith. Naturally this is not to say that the form of the law is Christian. For to say "Christian form" of the law necessarily means the form in which its religious power over man is broken. Instead of dominating him, it serves him. To speak of the law in its Christian form means that we *were* held in its custody, but *now,* in faith, it is no longer so, for "Christ is the end of the law" (Rom. 10:4). Considering that, Paul's assertion can be read without qualification: "All things are yours, whether . . . the world or life or death or the present or the future, all are yours." (I Cor. 3:21 f.) Thus in its Christian form the law has lost its religious power.

That does not mean that the law has become absolutely void. It means that in the religious sense, in reference to man's relation to God, it has lost the power of accusation and condemnation that it had for the pre-Christian man. It is incapable of shaking the Christian's certainty that nothing in the world can separate him from the love of God which is in Christ Jesus his Lord. (Rom. 8:31 ff.) The validity of the law is thus restricted to the objects and relations of the earthly world. To that extent, it is subordinated to the judgment of the human reason and it serves man in his independence toward the world. Now modern science, as we have seen, is by its own standards the methodically clearheaded explication of man's independence toward the world. In this world, deprived of the religious power of the law by the Christian faith, modern man exercises his independence in the knowledge of science and in the power it gives him access to. Hence, we can even say of the form of the law arrived at in this way that it is post-Christian. It serves to elaborate the Christian independence of man toward the world, the independence that was first made accessible by the Christian faith.

But we must speak in still another sense of the post-Christian character of this form of the law. The specifically Christian in the understanding of the law was lost when the methodically clearheaded elaboration of this independence no longer sufficed. Science therefore succumbed to the temptation to create a world view. Subjectivism was the outcome. For our concern in the discussion with subjectivism, it is of decisive importance to acknowledge clearly the nature and extent of this loss of the original understanding of the law. According to our present understanding, the specifically Christian in the meaning of the law is twofold: First is the loss of its religious power, based in the way faith understands the world and its powers in their creatureliness. Second is the independence of man toward the world and its law, which follows from the first. This independence has now lost the meaning it originally received from the Christian faith and has taken on a completely different meaning. The loss occurred when scientific thought tied itself to the subjectivistic world view. But something of importance must be noticed here. It is a peculiarity of modern scientific thinking that even though it has succumbed to the world view of subjectivism, in practice it follows its own methods. Hence, man's independence, in respect of the question of its actual achievement through scientific research and the power exercised in technology, is none other than that of a scientific mentality that has remained true to its own nature and true to the working out of the form of the law made accessible by the Christian faith and responsible to the reason. The meaning given this independence by the theory of the subjectivistic world view is quite different from the independence man actually achieved.

What is the nature of the change that took place here? To clarify it, we must remember that the depriving of the world and its laws of religious power in no way means they have been withdrawn from any positive relation to God. Wherever the Christian faith has remained true to itself it has never ceased to believe that the world as well as its law is God's creation. But it is just God's *creation*. The Christian faith is so exclusively faith in God the Creator that, to say it in the outline of the three articles of the Apostles' Creed, faith in Jesus Christ the Savior and in the Holy Spirit is likewise faith in the Creator. Only because that is so, can one be justified by faith alone without the works of the law. That means there is no other justification for man before God than comes from being God's creature. This is so, not simply in the sense that he was once created by God. Nor is it so, that once created by God he now lives by his own strength. Rather, as Luther expresses it, God's word, which is always the word of the Creator, " is continuously in vogue." Man, therefore, is never other than the one God created, called from nothing into being by God's creative word. He is, therefore, justified before God. Or, as we said earlier, he responds to God and can only respond to him since he responds as one called of God. That means that in faith he responds to God's creatorhood by giving himself. He responds with his whole creaturehood to God's creative word. Nothing but this faith can justify man before God. For only in it is man expectant toward God with his whole being. And because in this faith man entrusts himself to God's creative word, it is God the Creator who himself justifies man as his creature.

Not only does this faith allow man to be expectant toward God with his whole being. It also makes him aware of everything given him by which he can live his life as God's creature. Indeed, as we made clear earlier, that is the world God has granted him as his inheritance. He shall live in it as a mature son. In the independence into which he has thus been called, he can respond to the call of God with himself. This does not mean that he is called simply to " this or that." It means he is himself called, or, as we could also say, he is called to *the* faith in which he may be expectant toward the calling with his whole being. It would not have been possible for man to be expectant in this sense toward the creative call of God if he were in some way religiously bound through the world and its law, if these were for him something other than God's creation, which has no creative power of its own.

Man's independence toward the world and its law, then, as it is originally accessible in faith, is rooted in his creatureliness. The creaturely man responds in faith to the creatorhood of God and to the creaturehood of the world which is acknowledged in this response. This meaning of independence has undergone a fundamental change through the subjectivism of modern thought. For in subjectivism the base on which this very independence was founded has been lost. It is no longer known that man's independence has its source in the creatureliness of man and the world. Independence is now founded upon the prerogative of man " as a sub-ject who is distinguished because in an essential regard unconditioned " (Heidegger, *op. cit.,* p. 98) . Upon that prerogative " all being is founded in the manner of its being and its truth " (*ibid.,* p. 81) . But that means that the independence is now based on the nature of man himself. Hence, the creaturely man has become a being who can understand himself as man only on the basis of the claim that he is the source of meaning for all being. Yet, the greater the claim to being this creative source of meaning, the less is its creative power. It is not even adequate for an understanding of the world in its creatureliness. For since man has become " the relating center of being itself " (*ibid.,* p. 81) , the world has become his object. That means the world has become something that has its being by the fact that man " places it before himself and relates it to himself." And so the world is now " the product of the apprehending realization " for which man " can be the one being who gives all being its measure and applies the plumb line " (*ibid.,* p. 87) .

One will fully understand what happens here only if he remembers where this subjectivistic understanding of man's independence has its source. As we indicated earlier, modern scientific thinking was induced to gain its unrestricted freedom for research by struggling against the faith of the church. Indeed, that was a faith which no longer had the power to liberate the world and its law from religious worship. Hence, it was compelled to subject science for its own sake to the same law to which faith believed it had itself to submit. For because it was no longer the faith that alone justifies, it no longer had the power to believe that " all things are yours, whether . . . the world or life or death or the present or the future." With that faith, however, Paul and, fifteen hundred years later, Luther, who had come to maturity through that faith, delivered the world as God's creation over to man's reason.

13. A NEW UNDERSTANDING OF FAITH

The most appropriate task of faith is to safeguard man's freedom for God and therefore to deprive the world and its law of religious power. Faith is unable to do this unless it is ready to entrust the reason with working out man's independence toward the world and its law. This being the case, faith must not be averse to subjectivism because of its connotation of independence. For faith's own sake it must not. It would contradict itself. It would contradict its most proper task which only faith is able to fulfill and in whose fulfillment only does faith remain a justifying faith. In that way what led to subjectivism in the first place would only be repeated. It is not man's independence toward the world and the law in and for itself to which the Christian faith is opposed. Nor is it the form in which this independence has been methodically worked out in the course of modern times through scientific thinking. By " methodical " is meant " the rigor of research," led in each step by the idea of independence, which is valid not only in respect of the individual objects research has to validate but which is valid also on principle for the whole.

Certainly it must be observed that so methodically elaborated an independence did not occur to Luther or to the apostle Paul. In that sense it cannot be accounted for in terms of their understanding of faith. That does not exclude the possibility, however, that man's independence toward the world and its law, as it corresponds to their understanding of faith, is an independence of basically the same sort, comprehending, as it did, the whole of human existence and its possibilities as man's freedom for God, which they knew to be safeguarded by faith. It may even be surmised that this independence toward the whole of the world, methodically elaborated by modern scientific thinking, does not contradict faith; indeed, it presupposed faith understood as that which alone justifies. Hence, the task is set for understanding faith as man's freedom for God. Only in the defense of this freedom is faith a justifying faith. The consequence would be that faith would not contradict man's independence, the very independence that is just coming into prominence today in its whole range.

In our further considerations we must start from the twofold meaning of man's independence toward the world and its law. On the one side, it is an independence accessible only by faith. Hence, it remains accessible exclusively for and through faith. But then the independence is surrendered by faith to man's reason for elucidation. In regard to independence in this second sense, these words of the apostle Paul are appropriate: " 'All things are permitted,' but not all things are helpful " (I Cor. 10:23). In this statement the works of the law, which have no justifying power, are handed over to the free, reasonable decision of man. This freedom is already considerably more broadly developed by Luther than by Paul in Luther's doctrine of the " orders " (*ordines*) of human life. That being the case, we now ask whether man's independence, worked out by modern science in relation to the whole of the world through its methodical beginning, may not be of the same kind as the independence originally handed over by the Christian faith to the human reason for its free elaboration.

To answer this question, we attempted to clarify man's

relation to the world not only as it is accessible by faith but also as it remains accessible only in faith. As such, this relation corresponds immediately to man's freedom for God, which can be safeguarded only by faith. We found a Biblical expression for this relation in the concept of inheritance, meaning that the world is given over to the son who has come of age. This maturity, as we saw, obtains not only in relation to the world but in relation to God as well. For along with the world as the inheritance, God gives man at the same time the possibility of freedom for him. In man's relation to the world thus understood, there is the possibility of life in the world — indeed, a life in independence toward the world. But beyond that and prior to it is the possibility of life in the presence of God; hence, the independence of the mature son toward the father. The independence toward the world is based on the independence toward God. And the maturity of the heir toward the world has its measure in the maturity of the son before God, which is the filial freedom of man for God. Maturity in the presence of God embraces absolutely the entire existence of man. There is nothing that can qualify it. For whatever would qualify it would necessarily qualify God himself. If the possibility of his existence was first given man along with the world, it cannot be thought that the world becomes a limitation for man's existence. For it is the world which is granted to him, the mature son, as his inheritance. It is the world to which he is related in the independence of the " lord of all " (Gal. 4:1) and with which the possibility of filial freedom for God is given him. Just as there is nothing in the world that can qualify this freedom for God, so there is nothing that can limit man's freedom for the world, grounded as it is in the freedom for God.

Let us remind ourselves that man's freedom for God just as well as the corresponding independence toward the world exists only in faith. Hence, man's independence toward the world corresponds directly to faith. Without it faith does not exist as a faith that alone justifies. This independence as well as the freedom for God, then, has the reality appropriate to it only in faith. Considering the nature of this faith, that simply means that the slightest thought of " doing " or works as a means of achieving this independence must be kept as carefully at a distance as it would be in relation to freedom for God. The serious accomplishment of such a project is extraordinarily difficult for our customary theological and religious thinking. For, without knowing it or taking stock of it profoundly, in their understanding of faith they have fallen prey to modern thinking. Hence, they can understand the faith in scarcely any other than moral terms, as a " realizing-producing " faith (Heidegger, *op. cit.,* p. 82: *vorstellend-herstellenden*) . That is indicated with disconcerting clarity by the fact that our customary theological thinking, in spite of Paul and Luther, is so anxiously intent on nothing else as on this: to secure for faith the relation to reality that comes from thinking of it primarily in terms of its moral relevance. Thus it cannot fail to be obvious that faith, in spite of protests to the contrary and every sort of discourse about the Holy Spirit, is understood " as one possibility among others." Moreover, faith is regarded as a possibility that receives its vindication from the possibility of moral action. (Compare my essay " Glaube und Sittlichkeit in Luthers Schrift ' De servo arbitrio,' " in *Zeitschrift für Theologie und Kirche,* 1950, pp. 227 ff.) Do not misunderstand. The intention here is not to deny the relevance of faith for the doing of works. It is simply the intention to secure for faith the relevance appropriate to its nature.

What does it mean to say that the question of moral relevance must be kept separate from the question of the freedom for God and the corresponding independence toward the world that is accessible in faith? Positively expressed, it means that these freedoms must be considered in all their rigor and exclusiveness in relation to being. Only in this way is it meaningful to say that man by his sinfulness has subjected the creation of God to the nothingness and bondage of vanity and that therefore the same creation waits longingly for its deliverance through the revelation of the sons of God and their freedom. If this freedom and the sin annulled by it were considered only in relation to man's action, this other consideration would be completely incomprehensible. For action and works can engage only individual matters in the world, never the whole of the world. But what we are speaking of here pertains to the whole of the world as well as to the whole of man. Therefore, if the being of man and the world is a matter of this freedom and independence, then it is so only as this being can be recognized in faith.

This being is recognized when man becomes sensibly aware of the invisible nature of God, his eternal power and deity in this being as the work of creation. We have also seen previously that the awareness in which man appropriates this knowledge gets its meaning from the power man becomes aware of. What is valid for this power is what Luther had first recognized in relation to the righteousness of God and what became the unique cause of the Reformation. That was the knowledge that the Biblical expressions about God taken as a whole do not refer to God as a being in-and-for-himself but as a being related to the existence of man and the world. When the Bible says, as it does, for instance, in Ps. 85:7 (Vulgate), that God has turned toward us, it means that he makes it possible by his divine essence for us to turn toward him. (W.A. 4, 2.) Hence, as Luther says, those who are instructed in the Bible will understand that the works of God about which it speaks are none other than the works he performs in us. (W.A. 3, 54: *Inde eruditus concludit opera dei non esse, nisi quae deus in nobis operetur.*) A recognition of the works of God can be obtained, therefore, only as one who is aware of the divine power experiences it as the power that performs these works in him. Only in this way is one made aware of the power and deity of God " in its true meaning," or, as one could translate the Greek word *nooumena* in this place, " reasonably thought." This awareness of God's power and deity also engages the man's being. He becomes aware of his being as brought about in this awareness by God himself.

Such an awareness, which is effected when God in his invisible nature, his eternal power and deity, calls man out of nothing into being, is faith. Or faith is, as Paul says, in Gal. 4:9, the knowledge that occurs when man is known of God. Whatever happens in this awareness or in this knowledge is the reality with which faith is concerned, no more and no less. And this reality is the reality of God. But the reality of God is the reality of his " eternal power and deity " by which he calls what is not into being. If one were to believe that he could secure the relation of faith to reality by the " morally-realizing " procedure by which the theological and religious thinking of today is dominated, that effort would be met by the verdict Paul registered against the piety of the Gentiles and the Jews (Rom., chs. 1 and 2). For such a faith would be the same as this piety in the respect that it knew of God but had not safeguarded its knowledge of God, as these had not. For it did not glorify God " as " God. It sought the reality of God where the reality is not really God. Even of such a faith it could be said that it exchanges the reality of the incorruptible God for the reality of the corruptible man. That is, it exchanges the eternal power and deity of God for the moral capacity of man.

One can become aware of God's power and deity only in faith. So says Paul when he refers to the nature of God as " invisible." But " invisible " here does not simply mean that God is not visible in the perceptual sense. It means, moreover, that he is not accessible as a logical conclusion. The point is that one cannot conclude about God on the basis of something that is not God. If one tried to conclude about God's eternal power and deity in such a way, it would not be God who was known. One would only come in that way upon a God who belongs to the world, of the sort Paul refers to when he says, " There may be so-called gods in heaven or on earth — as indeed there are many ' gods ' and many ' lords ' " (I Cor. 8:5 f.; Paul is thinking of the cosmic powers) . Such a God would be, as these, only a creature and not the Creator. One could not worship him in truth " as " God. In other words, the eternal power and deity can be acknowledged only on its own basis, that is, on the basis of its power to call into being what was not. That is why God is called invisible and inaccessible. The working of this power is the being of man and the world as they are " from him and through him and to him " (Rom. 11:36) . The being of man and the world as they are purposed by God and his eternal power and deity is the being of the son who is free for God and the being of the world as the creation of God, entrusted to man in his filial maturity as an inheritance from God. That being is the reality that concerns faith. Man's task, which can be fulfilled only by him, is to safeguard this reality by being aware of it in the only way one is able to — by faith.

14. THE PREACHING OF JESUS AND BEING

We must now speak about how the faith in which reality is experienced is possible. By reality, of course, is meant that to which man's freedom for God and his independence toward the world correspond. It still needs to be made clear what is meant by saying that this faith is faith in Jesus Christ.

We have often said that it is impossible for man to recapture his forfeited sonship by his own power, just as it is impossible on one's own to restore the state of one's forfeited inheritance. Both can only be conferred on him anew. But faith in Jesus Christ is the belief that this event occurs through faith in Jesus Christ crucified and resurrected. Until now we have treated faith in detail without speaking explicitly of Jesus Christ. We have done so primarily to clarify the nature of this faith and, if I may say so, to clarify the range of experience within which it moves and within which it must therefore be seen. We tried to make it clear that this context is the being of God as well as of man and of the world. It was seen that the nature of faith is so completely determined through this being that its most unique task is to safeguard this being, since it in turn safeguards man's freedom for God. Only within this context can one understand how the lost sonship and lost inheritance are newly entrusted to men through faith in Jesus Christ. This is the redemption to be shared by men through faith in Christ. Such a context is no arbitrary notion to which the form of Jesus becomes a mere appendage. It is the context within which Jesus appeared on earth and in which faith has seen him from the beginning and which first became clear when Jesus appeared within it. Only because this has happened have we been able to speak of the context in the general terms we have used up to this point.

If theology is to be delivered from modern subjectivism, it is nowhere so important as in reference to the form of Jesus. Nowhere is such deep reflection required as it is here. For this form has become the object of subjectivism more than almost anything else in theology. When with the beginning of modern times the traditional metaphysics of late antiquity more and more disintegrated, the form of

Jesus Christ as outlined in theology became more and more untenable. This figure was thought out by means of Greek metaphysics, and for nearly fifteen hundred years of the Christian era was revered as the revelation of divine reality. In order not to lose Jesus completely, one had to try to understand him and his reality by means of the thought at one's disposal. The means, however, were the same as those framed under the influence of modern subjectivism. For about the last two centuries the form of Jesus has been cast in terms of subjectivism. The effort was quite successful. The metaphysical, dogmatized form of a heavenly Son of God became increasingly shadowy and unimpressive. In its place stepped the form of a historical man whose thoroughly human features one could recognize through the Gospel reports, especially those of the Synoptic Gospels. This development is particularly obvious in nontheological circles. One can more easily be emancipated from the old dogmatic tradition there than he can in theology, which is more tightly bound to the church. But in the course of time this trend has even operated with great force in theology and in the preaching of the church.

Therefore, the following statement could be printed in the first edition of the widely circulated work, *Die Religion in Geschichte und Gegenwart,* a Dictionary of Theological and Religious Knowledge: " One can certainly agree that within the Christian community the meaning and influence of Jesus Christ has at no time in the history of the church been greater than it is today." The basis and meaning of this astonishing sentence is explained in what follows: " This is connected in part with the German renaissance of the eighteenth century and the achievement of the personality culture of romanticism, in part with the intensive work by the theology of the nineteenth century in research on the life and self-consciousness of Jesus. The gains from all this have been passed on to the congregation through teaching and preaching." The meaning of these sentences is clear: the true significance of Jesus Christ was recognizable and his genuine historical influence possible only as his form was liberated from the religious, metaphysical interpretation of ancient Christian dogma which had made him a divine and heavenly essence far removed from man. Thus liberated, his true historical reality could again become clear.

Closely connected with this is the presupposition that the purely human reality of Jesus is of the type that could be understood with the help of idealist philosophy and classical and romantic poetry, and ultimately with the help of the historical concept of man as personality, expressed with the help of both philosophy and poetry. This means, however, that here man and thus the man Jesus of Nazareth is understood as a "realizing-producing" ("*vorstellend-herstellenden*") being, which is modern subjectivism's way of trying to understand man.

In the meantime, however, theological research had clearly shown this understanding of man to have miscarried when applied to Jesus. This manifested itself in the preaching and the claims that he placed before man in the name of God. With the understanding of man as the "realizing-producing" being, these commandments became completely meaningless, for understood in that way they are absolutely unrealizable. They are unrealizable not simply because the man of will and power fails to act in response to them. They are essentially incapable of being fulfilled if the fulfillment is of a type in which man understands the commandment as a realization of something he should do, and then accomplishes the realized deed. Even if he were actually to fulfill the commandment realized in this sense, he would in no way have done what Jesus' interpretation of the commandment required of him. Thus, for example, Jesus says: "You have heard that it was said to the men of old, 'You shall not kill; and whoever kills shall be liable to judgment.' But I say to you that every one who is angry with his brother shall be liable to judgment; whoever insults his brother shall be liable to the council, and whoever says, 'You fool!' shall be liable to the hell of fire." (Matt. 5:21 ff.)

One reduces a statement like that to harmlessness, and in an intolerable way, if one supposes that it is a sharpening of the meaning of the original commandment simply because instead of forbidding the external deed it forbids the inner anger. Something infinitely more and fundamentally different is required. Instead of acts or deeds, which could be done very well on the basis of a commandment, it requires of man a being. With that kind of being he could no longer have within him anger and insult for his brother; hence, murder would be out of the question. The claim of Jesus does not mean deeds, but being. That is illustrated by the statement about the good tree, which can bring forth fruit that is not evil. "Are grapes gathered from thorns, or figs from thistles?" (Ch. 7:16 ff.) Or still more clearly in the saying about alms: "When you give alms, do not let your left hand know what your right hand is doing, so that your alms may be in secret; and your Father who sees in secret will reward you." This saying clearly shows that the kind of alms required of him could not really have been given by command. For when given on the basis of a realization that is the law, it is utterly impossible to conceal from the left hand what the right hand is doing. Alms can be given in the required manner only by one who is compassionate and who therefore helps one who is in need without consideration of whether a command has been given that requires alms.

The reason that the demands of Jesus relate to the being of man and not to his action is that he understands them as the demand God puts on man. God's demand, however — and it is also possible to read his individual commands in the same way — is utterly single: to love the

Lord with your whole heart and mind and strength. That means no more and no less than that man should belong to God with his whole being, receiving himself in his being from God, his Lord. The " being from God " is received in faith. That presupposition makes it possible to understand the essence of the command as meaningful. The claim is fulfilled by participation in the " rewards of your father in heaven " (ch. 6:1). The " being from God " is what Jesus preached. The meaning of his whole preaching is to tell man how his being is constituted, what its constitution is, and to call him into this being.

In what way does Jesus' preaching call one into this being? How does he intend that participation in this being is possible for the man he addresses? The answer is clear when it is known that Jesus understands this very preaching as happening from being. This is the difference between his preaching and that of the Old Testament prophets. Jesus preached the call of God just as the prophets did. But Jesus did it by preaching himself. So whether one participates in the " being from God " depends on how one relates himself to Jesus. In the answer to the question John the Baptist puts to Jesus as to whether he is the One who should come, Jesus first of all repeats the Old Testament preaching. But he concludes with a word no Old Testament prophet had said or could have said: " Blessed is he who takes no offense at me." (Ch. 11:6.) If Jesus preached God's call by preaching himself, that does not mean he held himself up as the example for the hearing of the divine call. Nor does it mean that he regarded himself as one to whom this call did not pertain as it did to other men.

God's call, which Jesus heard for himself in the same way as all others should hear it, now summons man. It calls man to be and to be on the basis of being called. That means God calls man to be where He calls. Jesus' preaching stems from the hearing of this call. Because that is so, hearing and being where God calls are heard in the preaching of Jesus as God's own call. In this way, every man is able to participate in the being from God by hearing Jesus' preaching. That is the significance of his call to discipleship. Discipleship means infinitely more than that one should follow Jesus as an example for his own action. It means this immediate participation in the being that has become manifest in Jesus and in his preaching.

The preaching of Jesus as well as Jesus himself as preacher must be understood in relation to this being. His preaching both originates in it and makes it accessible. With reference to Jesus, all the religio-moral categories by which one attempts to understand Jesus and his preaching break down. With the dwindling of the religio-metaphysical dogmas of the early church, the "realizing-producing" thinking of subjectivism has come into dominance in theology. But this being is no better understood as a "realizing," in the sense of a command, than it was on the basis of metaphysical dogma. For this being is itself the presupposition of every command. Whoever realizes this being as a command falls hopelessly short of it. Nor may one realize being in the sense of "producing" it. If a command is to have any meaning for this being, it can demand no less than the "turning about" from all prior action to this being as the "origin" of all the realization that is asked of man.

15. BEING AND THE APOSTOLIC PREACHING

In the apostolic preaching of the New Testament the person and the work of Jesus were understood as integrally related to his being. In order to make this relationship clear, we shall examine a short passage from Rom., ch. 8, in which Paul speaks in a highly concentrated way of the redeeming work of Jesus Christ. " There is therefore now no condemnation for those who are in Christ Jesus. For the law of the Spirit of life in Christ Jesus has set me free from the law of sin and death. For God has done what the law, weakened by the flesh, could not do: sending his own Son in the likeness of sinful flesh and for sin, he condemned sin in the flesh, in order that the just requirement of the law might be fulfilled in us, who walk not according to the flesh but according to the Spirit." (Rom. 8:1-4.)

The most important concepts in this statement are " flesh " and " Spirit." It is said that the man who walks " according to the flesh " incurs sin and death. On the other hand, if he walks " according to the Spirit " he becomes a partaker of the life that was made manifest in Jesus Christ. At the same time, it is said of Jesus Christ that he is closely related not only to the " Spirit " but also to the " flesh." He is the One in whom the law of the Spirit lives and does its work of freedom. But it also says that God has sent him, his Son, " in the form of sinful flesh." Finally, both the law of the " Spirit " and the law of the " flesh " are mentioned. But it is not immediately clear whether Paul is speaking about two different laws, or about one and the same law, which can then be a law of the " flesh " as well as of the " Spirit."

We have already seen the complexity of Paul's concept of the " flesh." It denotes not only " flesh " in the narrower sense — that is, the immediate, inherent awareness of being alive — but also the world, and man in his relation to the world, for both have arisen through the sin of man — the choosing of the creature instead of the Creator. The world and man have thereby undergone a fateful perversion. The crucial point is that man has forfeited his filial responsibility for the world as the inheritance granted him. In this way, both the world and man with his responsibility for the world are subjected to "nothingness." This "nothingness," as we have seen, is an annihilating nothingness. That is to say, it is not only a condition or state, but rather an active, effective power. The means of its annihilating power is the law in the form it takes on for the man who, by his own choice, places his trust in the creature instead of in the Creator. Paul calls the law in this form the "law of sin and death." For these two, sin and death, are the truly annihilating powers under which man and his world have fallen as a result of his forfeited responsibility.

We are now also able to understand what Paul means when he speaks of man's "walking" according to the "flesh" or according to the "Spirit." This is usually understood "as designating the conduct of life, particularly in its moral aspect" (*Theologisches Wörterbuch zum Neuen Testament,* Vol. III, p. 944). But in this instance, in any case, it means much more than that. "Flesh" and "Spirit" are understood here as powers that have authority over man's being. The "flesh," whose life is incessantly threatened by its inherent transitoriness, exercises its power because it holds man's reflection about his life tightly in the annihilating power of its own nothingness. The "Spirit" is called "life-giving" because it opens to man the freedom for God which calls into being that which is not. Man's "walking," therefore, refers in its true meaning not only to man's ethical or unethical way of living. Rather, as a "walking according to the flesh" it means man's being as it is under the fate of forfeited sonship and its responsibility, in which the "law of sin and death" rules over him; as a "walking according to the Spirit" it means the freedom of man as of a son for God, in which he is saved from the power of that law through the power of the "life-giving Spirit."

We can now try to clarify what Paul is saying about Jesus Christ in this passage, and thus how walking "according to the flesh " is redemptively transformed through him into walking " according to the Spirit." It happens this way, Paul says: God, since he sent his Son on account of sin in the " form of flesh and of sin," condemned sin in the flesh, that the demand of the law might be fulfilled in us, who walk no longer " according to the flesh but according to the Spirit." First of all, let us ask about the meaning of " the Son in the form of flesh and of sin." This statement contains an enormous contradiction. Two different things are said of the One to whom these words refer. On the one hand, he is the " Son of God," and on the other, he is sent " in the form of flesh and of sin." Two statements which stand in the deepest and most irreconcilable contradiction are made here with reference to one and the same person. The wholeness of man's being as a son of God is here, and the forfeited sonship is also here. Man's whole being as son of God contains in itself the whole being of the world as God's creation and as the inheritance in which God's being as father and creator continues. Therefore, Paul says, " God sent his Son in the form of flesh and of sin " — which is to say, According to God's will, there has been born into the world One who, like all in this world, was subjected to the guilt-laden destiny that hangs over all men and their world as a consequence of the sinful exchange of Creator for creature. This destiny is laid upon him because he is one of us, " born of woman, born under the law " (Gal. 4:4). But what does Paul mean when he says that God sent his own " Son " into the world? In order not to lose the force of the thought Paul has here, one must guard against conceiving of this " Son " as a sort of heavenly being, the Redeemer of Gnostic times. Easy edification is only too ready to represent him in that way today. One can understand Paul's statements only by keeping the whole contradiction intact. Without the contradiction Paul's statements would lose their meaning, because the name " Son of God " in the Christian faith applies not only to this One but to all men together.

God has created as sons those who should live before him in mature responsibility for the inheritance bestowed on them, which is the world. So he " predestined [them] to be conformed to the image of his Son, in order that he might be the first-born among many brethren " (Rom. 8:29) . But men have forfeited this form of the Son. As we have seen, this does not mean that they have ceased to be sons of God. So the sending of the Son in the " form of flesh and of sin " means that the One to whose form and sonship men should be conformed has assumed the form of the son as it has been forfeited by them. Paul also tells us by what power this has been accomplished. It has been done out of the power of the " law of the life-giving Spirit," which is, as Paul says in another verse in the same chapter, the " spirit of sonship." Or, as we can also say, it is his being as a son. What this means is that a son, if he is really a son, feels and knows with his whole being that what he is comes from the father, and that everything which comes to him comes from the father. It must not be overlooked that being as a son includes being as a brother. It includes responsibility with the brothers for the world, for their common inheritance. This filial being knows it is supported and upheld by the gift of the father, sent to it in the inheritance to the brothers. Being and remaining a son and carrying out the responsibility of a son lets the One take upon himself as his own the guilt-laden fate of the disastrous perversion of being to which the world and the brothers are held captive.

Because this One takes upon himself the guilt-laden fate by no other means except through the power of his being as son and brother, nourished by God's being the father, that fate is turned. And here our passage distinctly says how that happens. Because God sends his Son into the world in the " form of flesh and of sin," he speaks his judgment upon " sin in the flesh." Now a judge may condemn an offense only after it has been disclosed as an offense. We have seen, however, that what makes the exchanging of creature and Creator, with which the fate of perverted being came upon men and their world, into an ordained destiny, and therefore into an event that can never be undone but that runs its course irresistibly, is the fact that sin perverts even the law, and to such an extent that the law is no longer able to provide the knowledge of sin. For sin, as Paul has said shortly before (Rom. 7:13), has, "in order that it might be shown to be sin and sinful beyond all measure, worked death in me through the good, that is, the commandment." [RSV: "It was sin, working death in me through what is good, in order that sin might be shown to be sin, and through the commandment might become sinful beyond measure."] Paul now says that God has "condemned sin in the flesh," and then he says that God by his judgment has lifted up and disclosed this perversion, since through his judgment sin in its own most powerful manifestation has been unveiled.

This unveiling occurs through the death of Jesus Christ on the cross. To be sure, Paul does not say so explicitly in this passage. But he does not need to. For "the crucified Christ" (I Cor. 1:23) is the One to whom all of Paul's words refer, without exception. It is in this — that the Christ is the crucified One — that the true "form of flesh and of sin," in which the Father has sent his Son, becomes visible. We must remember that for Paul the cross is the sign of the divine curse. "Cursed be every one who hangs on a tree." Paul quotes that from Deuteronomy (ch. 21:23) in Galatians (ch. 3:13). And so he makes the tremendous statement about the crucified Christ: "He has become a curse for us." (Gal. 3:13.)

Now only he who can bless can curse. So, for example, a father, by his own fatherly word, the word in which his fatherhood is articulated, is able to bestow on the son his being as a son in the word in which he promises himself to the son as father. But with the same fatherly word, in withholding himself as father from his son, he may deny his very sonship. Such is the curse of the blessing when it is perverted into its opposite. So Paul says of the crucified Christ that he has become a curse for us. Then he says that God, because he sent him into the world in the "form of flesh and of sin," has spoken in him and upon him the curse with which he denies himself to men as father and to their world as creator. The ground of his denial is the sin of man. The perversion of the divine blessing into the condemning curse, which was brought about by sin, was taken upon himself by the crucified One. Thus the cross is a twofold sign of the divine curse. Through the cross the judgment upon sin is both pronounced and carried out.

But with this not everything that takes place through the crucified One is yet accounted for. The cross of Christ for the Christian faith is not only the disclosure of the guilt-laden fate of perverted being that lies upon man and his world. It is at the same time the turning of this fate. It must be understood why Christendom's cross of Christ is not only the sign of the divine judgment upon man and his world but is also the sign of the salvation brought to man by the crucified One. Great care must be taken to avoid rendering the above statements innocuous, as is so easily done, when it is said with the New Testament that these statements are one. This oneness can be understood rightly only if the antithesis is recognized in all its sharpness. The apostolic preaching asserts the oneness of the opposition of death and life, of evil and redemption, of the crucified Jesus and the resurrected Jesus. If this is not recognized, all talk of the resurrection and the salvation revealed in it becomes loose spiritual chatter affirming an empty, arbitrary belief. To speak of the resurrected Christ as one who is not also the crucified One, in the full Biblical sense of the divine curse upon the world and men, is to indulge in wishful thinking that has no reality.

What takes place on the cross can be comprehended only if it is grasped as the revelation of God, who speaks his complete divine judgment upon the perversion of his creation, both of the sons and of the world, and on the resultant forfeiture of being under the bondage of nothingness. That is God's condemning judgment, his curse upon everything that is. This judgment, indeed, falls first upon the One who, sent " in the form of flesh and of sin," took upon himself the last full measure of guilt. " He was obedient." (Phil. 2:8.) By that the apostle Paul means, " Yea, obedient unto death on a cross." This judgment would have no object or meaning if it did not at the same time pass sentence upon those who caused the guilt, in that they forfeited the form of sonship for which they were destined, and perverted it into its opposite, into " the form of flesh and of sin." In other words, the event that has been given the name of the cross does not concern only the one man who suffered his own bodily death upon it. Rather, just in the way it proclaims God's condemning judgment on far more than the bodily death, it concerns the whole world of men. For it is the death of the world, and in this death the annihilating revelation of the wrath of God appears as it " is revealed from heaven against all ungodliness and wickedness of men who by their wickedness suppress the truth " (Rom. 1:18).

" Wrath of God " does not mean merely an emotional impulse that can pass away as it came. It means the deity of God as it is for the one who has denied that deity and in so doing has forfeited everything that comes to him from the deity, perverting it into its opposite. In order to grasp what Paul is saying here in its full profundity, one must realize that the knowledge of the reality of God's wrath is not accessible to us men who view it from afar in the nakedness and authority in which it is meted out to the crucified One. For, to say he is " the crucified Christ " means, first of all, that through an unclouded awareness of a kind we are incapable of, he knew what happened because of the guilt-laden fate of perverted being, and in the obedience of a son and a brother took upon himself as his own the " form of flesh and of sin." Although intended in another sense perhaps, what Paul says at the close of the thirteenth chapter of I Corinthians applies here: " We see as in a mirror dimly, and not, as later, face to face; we know only in part, and not as we are known." But even this dimly apprehended knowledge stands under the condition that we, who are in the " form of flesh and of sin," recognize our true form, our forfeited sonship, as it was sent into our world and made visible for all the world on the cross. If the knowledge of the deity of God revealed for us on the cross is only a partial knowledge, it is nevertheless a true knowledge. To be sure, it is totally different from the knowledge, if I may say so, of a domesticated God. One would perhaps do best to avoid predication of God, simply because the predication would pertain to real knowledge of God. Whereas one might, rather, speak of the power beyond predication, before which a man who despairs in himself sees everything that had given his life sure support and meaning disappear into unreality, and which stands over against him as a dark and threatening power before which he cannot stand.

If what takes place on the cross is not only the revealing of the guilty fate of the perversion of being, but is at the same time the turning of this fate, then that must mean that on the cross the forfeited sonship is bestowed anew. For the sonship to be forfeited, and for that fate to come over man and his world, it is decisive that man declines the fatherly promise of God. In so doing, he falls into an unredeemable debt toward God. For what he owed to God is himself. Between man and God there stands the debt of man's forfeited sonship, and so of his forfeited inheritance, the world as God's creation. If the cross is the turning of this fate, that can mean nothing less than that on the cross this debt is redeemed. If that had not taken place, the newly bestowed sonship could never have been true sonship. It could never have been the sonship of a mature son, mature in relation to God as well as to the world. The debt could only be redeemed if the nothingness to which human existence is subject through that debt exercises its destructive power to the bitter end. For only as man becomes as nothing can he participate in sonship again. As John's Gospel expresses it, only then can man be born again.

We said above that the sentence " God sent his Son in the form of flesh and of sin " contains an enormous contradiction. The contradiction is that two things have happened in the one person of Jesus: the most extreme annihilation and being " designated Son of God in power," as Paul says in Rom. 5:15, " the free gift in grace." The same thing is signified in the Christian belief in Christ as the crucified and risen One. What the New Testament calls cross and resurrection pertains to two forms of knowledge of God, opposed to each other in the highest way and mutually exclusive. Only when both these forms of knowledge are thought through in their full significance, and each held firmly in its truth, is the one knowledge possible which they proclaim in their contradiction. That means that only when it is understood that the annihilating power, revealed in the death of Jesus Christ on the cross, is of such a kind that the bodily death is by far the least significant thing that occurs through it — only when that is understood can one grasp what happens in the resurrection.

The resurrection does not mean just the return of a dead man to life. It means infinitely more. It means that he who in his death on the cross descended to the lowest depths of perverted being has been lifted up to the highest level of divine Sonship. It means that God has given to the One whom he sent into the world in the " form of flesh and of sin " the name " which is above every name, that at the name of Jesus every knee should bow, in heaven and on earth and under the earth, and every tongue confess that Jesus Christ is Lord, to the glory of God the Father " (Phil. 2:9-11) . The resurrection means the revelation and the knowledge of God. In the most outward and total annihilation, understandable only in his eternal judgment as a judgment that sues for the debt of the whole world and before which everything comes to naught, God lets the power of his life be made manifest in the One who comes to nothing before him.

We said that the cross and the resurrection of Jesus Christ offer two opposing forms of the awareness of God, both of which are true and must be firmly held. We can now single them out. The knowledge of the cross is the knowledge of the eternal wrath of the hidden God, whose unveiled face no man can see and live. The knowledge of the resurrection is the knowledge of eternal salvation and life, which is the counterpart of the annihilating wrath. The relation between them, the *proportio,* according to a statement by Luther, is such that they are like each other. The wrath and death are unbounded, and the mercy and life are likewise unbounded. (Compare Luther, W.A. 40, 577.) The mercy is not limited by the wrath. The one reality of God is in both, and it is this reality which faith recognizes in the contradiction. Therefore, it can be said of this faith that it unites what is self-contradictory (*fides conciliat contraria*) . It is no longer true, then, that " in the midst of life we are in death " (*media vita in morte sumus*) , but rather that " in the midst of death we are in life " (*media morte in vita sumus*) (W.A. 43, 219) .

16. LUTHER'S UNDERSTANDING OF FAITH AND THE WORD

According to Luther, both condemnation and salvation pertain to the whole of man and his world. Either man's being and the being of the world is fallen because of nothingness, or that being is life lived "from and through God" (Rom. 11:36). Either man's being is condemned or it is saved. Either it is without wholeness or it is whole. There is thus a double infinity. As Luther expressed it, the reality both of the unsaved being and of the saved being embraces the whole. Jesus lived and finished his work within just such a context.

Now Luther says of faith that it "unites opposites." This is so because faith believes in One in whom condemnation and salvation, death and life are united. He is the One sent by God "in the form of flesh and sin." In the responsibility of a son he took upon himself the destiny of being's perversion as his own destiny. He persevered through the ultimate depths of guilt and thereby turned the drift of being. When is this faith, then, real faith in the Son sent by God, and when does it unite the opposites which have become manifest in their unity through this Son? Faith is real when one acknowledges that the "form of flesh and of sin" and the destiny assumed by the One sent in this likeness is our own guilty destiny. Faith is real when in this acknowledgment one participates in the being of the Son sent by God, who has had mercy for his brothers because he is the obedient Son.

One certainly cannot fail to see it as a confession when Paul says that God has sent "his own Son in the form of sinful flesh and for sin . . . in order that the just requirement of the law might be fulfilled in us, who walk not according to the flesh but according to the Spirit" (Rom. 8:3-4). For in this statement Paul confesses that this form is his own and that therefore he is guilty of the destiny of the disastrous perversion of being that the One whom God sent has taken upon himself. What is involved here is not a confession to a moral transformation. It is, rather, the confession of participation in the being of Jesus Christ. Hence, in Christ crucified and risen the condemned and saved being becomes one. By this confession faith derives its meaning and its essence from the One believed in. The kind of faith it is and the way the believer participates in the event of faith can best be explained in terms of Luther's understanding of faith.

The Christian faith believes exclusively in the event that takes place in and with the person of Jesus Christ. For Luther that is self-evident. It is just as evident for him that faith is not yet faith when it believes in the historically factual occurrence of these events. "To do so does not help," he says, "because sinners believe in that sense, even the damned sinners. Regarding that kind of belief, the Scripture and the word of God teach nothing; that is a natural work, without grace." The properly gracious faith that God's word and work require is much more — "that you believe firmly that Christ is given you and that his birth has occurred for your good" (W.A. 10, I_1, 71). Wherever that is not believed, one is apt to make the mistake of the scholastic theologians and the fathers, too, who made Christ into a "private person," "holy and righteous for himself alone." One ought not to stop at that. For it does not yet bring one to Christ, and hence one would not yet bear Christ's name. Only "when this most innocent person is given to men, so that he becomes my King and my priest, serves me, sheds his holiness and wills to be a sinner, saying I will suffer for you — there the Christ begins." (W.A. 40, I, 188.)

The true faith for Luther, therefore, is not a matter of holding historical facts as true. But neither is it a matter of holding theological beliefs as true. " Christ is called the Christ not because he has a human and a divine nature, but because of the office and work he has assumed and not because he has assumed flesh and blood." (W.A. 16, 217.) The true faith, rather, rests entirely on the expression " for us " (W.A. 40, I, 448). Only when the pronoun " our " is emphasized in every article of faith — conceived for us, born for us, suffered for us, risen for us, ascended for us, sitting at the right hand for us " (W.A. 34, II, 509) — is the event called Christ really apprehended by faith. It is this " for me, for us, which constitutes true faith when it is believed, and distinguishes it from that other faith which stops with the events which have happened " (W.A. 39, I, 46). The " proper basis for acknowledging the suffering of Christ," therefore, is " when one rightly acknowledges and grasps not only his suffering but his heart and will to suffering " (W.A. 17, II, 173). The proper event is indicated by every pronoun " our, we, us, which we should inscribe in gold letters " (W.A. 31, II, 432). The event is not simply the " what " but the " why " of the history. (W.A. 27, 105.) Therefore, one should not scorn these pronouns. One must hold them fast, and thus be among those for whose sins Christ has been given. " This faith justifies you and makes it possible for Christ to live and rule in you. And this faith is the witness of the Spirit which witnesses with our spirit that we are sons of God. If you are attentive, you will easily observe that this aspect is not in you as a result of powers of your own. Therefore, it is obtainable only through a humble spirit which despairs of itself." (W.A. 2, 458.)

From what has been said, it is clear that the event in which the Christian faith believes, according to Luther's understanding, is no so-called objective event. At least, it is not the kind of event man realizes as a spectator and to which he then produces a relation, however constituted. Rather, this is the kind of event in which man is " intended " from the outset and into which he is taken up. In this sense Luther speaks of the *usus,* " the use of history." If one knows nothing of the use of history, history is meaningless. In that case faith has nothing to do with it. One should not overlook the fact that the word " use " for Luther has a double meaning. Basically there is a meaning that the modern reader probably seldom detects. He usually understands it in the ordinary sense, that is, the use man makes of the event. Luther, of course, understands the word in this way too, but with the important difference that for him another meaning is presupposed in this understanding which changes its ordinary meaning. Before Luther thinks about the use man makes of the event, he has already thought of the use Christ or God makes of it. It therefore becomes clear that he distinguishes between the " what " (*quid*) of the event and the infinitely more important " why " (*qua re*). In the " why " he sees " the use for the sake of which the history should be heard " (W.A. 27, 104). As he says in relation to the resurrection of Jesus Christ, one must " be careful to understand what it means to you and what he means by it " (W.A. 17, I, 184). The same thinking is expressed in relation to the Passion of Christ when Luther says one may be stimulated " to behold the Passion of Christ no longer (for that has now done its work and terrified you), but rather to penetrate and behold his friendly heart, how full of love it is toward you to compel him to bear your conscience and your sin so heavily. Thus your heart sweetens toward him and the trust of faith strengthens. Thereafter, ascend through Christ's heart to the heart of God and behold that Christ would not have had such love for you if God in his eternal love had not willed to have it. In his love for you Christ is obedient to that eternal love." (W.A. 2, 140.)

The " use " which Christ or God makes of the event in which faith believes is the " meaning," the intention, or the will by which they allow this event to occur. And this " intention " points to the man for whose sake they do it. The " use " man should make of the event and by which he comprehends it in its proper meaning must correspond precisely to this divine use. But that is only possible because man is intended by Christ and God in this use, or, to say it another way, because in consequence of this intention, he is already in this event. Thus Luther can say in his " Sermon on the True Meditation Over the Passion of Christ " that one who does not learn to have compassion on himself has missed the Passion of Christ. For " you are a fool if, while Christ mourns and suffers for you, you walk along in security about yourself as if you need any the less to have compassion on yourself. For is not Christ's compassion quite a personal matter for you, so that his mourning is for your sake, and your mourning means not yours but his? Whoever does not acknowledge himself and find himself in Christ's Passion does not sufficiently acknowledge that Passion. His suffering together with Christ is in vain." (W.A. 1, 338 f.) To say that the human " use " of this event should correspond to its divine " use " can only mean that man through faith should be aware before all else of this divine " intention " in the event. For whatever else may happen in it, the event occurs for the sake of this " intention " and only for that. Only in this " intention " does the event have its power.

Throughout his entire life Luther had called this divine " intention " the " word " of God. For him everything hinged on this " word." The reason was that in the word as nowhere else the " intention " was powerful and apparent. Once early in his life he expressed it that way — and it is also the seed of his later doctrine of the sacrament: " understood in the light of the gospel, all words, all stories, are sacraments, that is, signs through which God works in the believers what these histories signify." "If one hears the story of Christ and does not believe that it means me, that Christ is born in me [in the sense Luther shortly thereafter states, namely, that I am thereby reborn], has suffered for me, and has died for me, then the preaching or the knowledge of the story of Christ is useless." (W.A. 9, 440.) In this sense one must understand the gospel with all its words and stories as sacrament. For only then will one recognize that this word does for us by faith what they are talking about. (W.A. 9, 442.) Therefore, in the event in which one believes, everything depends on the word. For what should happen along with the word is brought about only in the word. Hence, if faith is to be true, it must correspond to the word of the event. "For the works of God are his words, because the action and speech of God are the same thing." (W.A. 3, 152.) This is what Luther means when he says that one should know no God and Christ except the One he knows in the word. (W.A. 36, 45.) For because "Christ has held himself to the word," "we should see to it that we abide by the Scripture, or we will never grasp it, either with the hand or with our thoughts and spirit." (W.A. 27, 16.)

In customary theology there is an understanding of the "word" of God roughly parallel to the entitling of a picture by the painter. The painter puts a name under his picture so the public can recognize what the picture "should mean" without putting a strain on the public's powers of observation. When this tactic is found in theology it can be explained by the domination of subjectivistic thinking. The more real the practice is, the less aware one is of it. For this kind of thinking wants the objective reality in the word of God understood in such a way, lest everything dissolve for it into subjectivistic relativism. The recent intensive treatment of Luther's theology has changed hardly anything in this unusual and amazingly primitive understanding of the "word." (This, incidentally, is not true of the confessional Lutherans alone.) For instance, Luther has said God does not act apart from the word. He does not even deal with man except through the word of promise. Hence, we can never deal with God except by faith in his word of promise. (W.A. 6, 516: Remarks of this kind can be found not only in obscure places but in all his writings, in fact, in innumerable quantities at every epoch in his life. I have cited primarily from one of his best-known writings, *The Babylonian Captivity of the Church,* 1520.) If that is so, it is not difficult to see that this " word " of promise has in no sense the connotation of a title or name such as the painter gives to his picture. Rather, it is a word by which something is " done." This word does not simply speak about something. It immediately brings to pass what it announces. For God " through his promise is the author of our salvation, so that everything hinges on the word of his power through which he has begotten us and everything is carried and conserved by that word " (W.A. 6, 514).

The faith that is given in marriage with the word very closely corresponds to Luther's understanding of the word (W.A. 37, 175). This faith would not be consummated if one were to understand it simply as an act of accepting a statement as true. A truly creative faith perceives the word by allowing the event to occur that happens immediately in and with the perception of the word. Then for the first time it becomes " clear that the entrance and origin of our salvation is the faith that rests on the word of the promising God. God comes to us without any effort on our part in pure grace and unmerited mercy and offers us the word of his promise." (W.A. 6, 514.) " One cannot seize the word with anything, neither with his hands, feet, nor with the whole body, but only with the heart, with faith." In order to say clearly what that means, Luther must add that " therefore outwardly everything is blameworthy and must be crucified, slandered, and insulted. Only faith is irreproachable. God looks with favor only on it and on what is in it" (W.A. 10, III, 271 f.). The word of God is a promising word. It is indeed the word in and with which God promises himself as the One who "makes the dead alive." What the word promises happens in and with it, for in it God binds himself to man with the whole fullness of his deity, that man "may live in the life in which God lives" (W.A. 43, 221). This being so of the word, Luther can say of the faith that believes in this word that it is "nothing but the true life in God himself" (W.A. 44, 717).

Inasmuch as God gives us life by his word, we can give God what he requires of us by faith in this word. But he does not require our works. With works we can only do something toward men and with them and ourselves. But he requires that we regard him as true in his promises and in his patience, worshiping him in this way in faith, hope, and love. For it so happens that in us he retains his glory. We have and receive every good thing not through our activity but only through his mercy, promise, and gift (W.A. 6, 516). He requires our faith in order, as Luther would say, to be our God. But he is our God in the word in which he promises himself to us. Because the word of God to which faith responds is of this kind, Luther can boldly assert that faith is "the creator of deity." In order not to be misunderstood, Luther immediately adds what is self-evident for him, that God is in this way created "not in his person but in us. Outside faith God loses his righteousness, honor, power, etc., and where there is no faith nothing remains of his glory and deity." (W.A. 40, I, 360. *Fides est creatrix divinitatis, non in persona, sed in nobis. Extra fidem amittit deus suam iustitiam, gloriam, opes, etc., etc nihil majestatis, devinitatis, ubi non fides.*)

The word of God, then, is of the sort just explained. In it his action with man, as it occurs in the life and Passion of Christ, is "comprised," according to Luther's formulation. Faith corresponds with this word. If that is clear, one may understand that what happens between this word and this faith concerns being, the being of God as well as the being of man. Only because this is so can Luther make the claim that faith is " the creator of deity." For it asserts that faith, immediately taken up with the being or nonbeing of man, and even with man's capacity for being or nonbeing before God, has to do immediately with the being of God. Whoever believes can " stand " before God. Whoever does not, cannot. For whoever believes responds to God's deity, his " eternal power and deity " in which he calls into being that which is not. Whoever does not believe denies himself to God's deity and thereby in this act denies to God his deity. Hence, faith is the " creator " of the deity " in us." For faith alone grants to God what he requires of us: the honor of his deity. " When God has his deity unviolated and uninjured, then he has what I can give him." (W.A. 40, I, 360.) God requires his deity of us. He requires that we allow him to be God in us in his unreduced and unviolated deity. " In us," of course, must be interpreted in Luther's sense. We must let him be " our God," " for us." Only in this way does faith respond to " the use " that God will make of man, since he reveals himself to man as the One who makes the dead alive.

Were it otherwise with the word and the faith, the apostle Paul could never have said what he did about faith and about man in the presence of God: " Therefore we conclude that a man is justified by faith without the works of the law." For faith would be one work alongside others. But true faith in Luther's sense is faith that responds to the word in which God promises the believer not only " this or that " but his very being as God. If that is true, one can understand Luther's bold word about faith without any difficulty. He can even recognize that it has not the slightest to do with subjectivism, a fact that indeed must remain hidden to subjectivistic thinking. For subjectivism must be on the lookout for an objective reality, simply because it is subjectivistic. That does not obtain here, however. It could only do so in relation to God if there were any possibility of settling the matter of his reality without its concerning us. But it always concerns us, because it pertains originally to our being and concerns us as wrath or mercy. For wrath and mercy are the whole being of God as it intends man, as the words already cited from Luther say concerning the infinity of wrath and mercy. Hence, wrath and mercy concern us in our whole being. " Whoever is under wrath is wholly under it, and whoever is under mercy is wholly under it, because wrath and mercy intend the person." (W.A. 8, 106.) And the mercy and wrath of God intend the being or nonbeing of man. Therefore, there is no neutral possibility between or alongside them. In this alternative of the mercy or the wrath of God and the related alternative of the being or nonbeing of man, faith is concerned with the being of God and the being of man. Hence, as we saw earlier, it is the proper task of faith, realizable by it alone, to safeguard the freedom of man for God. When faith fulfills this task, it is justifying faith. But only then.

Luther says that genuine faith does not direct itself to historical facts (*historie*), the " res," the " what " of the event but to the " use," the " why " of the event, or the " word " in which the event is " comprised." In the same way we can say that only justifying faith may comprehend the event in its proper reality. Knowledge of the " objective " historicity of the Christ event surely does not make for true faith, but only the knowledge that Christ is the One who justifies. For " the knowledge or the use and usefulness of Christ is for faith nothing else than that he has taken my sin upon himself and has strangled it through his resurrection. By this faith one can recognize Christ in the right way. Otherwise one does not know him." (W.A. 9, 555.) This knowledge, however, can never be proved by a so-called objective event. Nor can such proof be subsequently invoked. For such a proof of the event neutralizes it, putting it away, so to speak, in a neutral sphere where it could be known without faith. A so-called faith-knowledge of these " objective " facts can naturally be quite orthodox theologically. This is probably because in most cases of this sort faith comes from the knowledge of dogma and is nothing but " believed " dogma. But such a faith-knowledge does not even base itself upon the Christ event. One must say with Luther that faith of this kind is " a natural work without grace."

The event, therefore, in which the Christian faith believes, responding to it in the original sense of the word, is a word-event, an event happening in and through the word. Rather than refer to it as verbal, we could speak of it as personal. That is, it can be said that it is an event that in a real sense occurs between persons, hence through and in persons. Because Luther has understood the event between God and man in this way, he has understood the God-relation in a Biblical sense and has restored to faith its central and controlling meaning.

The God-relation is already comprehended in purely personal terms in the Old Testament, even though the human partner is still not the individual as it is in the New Testament but the people, the individual being only a member of the " chosen " people. Jahweh promises himself, or as Hosea has expressed it, Jahweh betroths himself to the people as their God. And Israel corresponds to this covenant when it remains in the trust and love, in the righteousness and in the mercy in which Jahweh has chosen Israel as his people. (Compare my book *Die Verkündigung Jesu Christi,* pp. 51 ff.) The Temple worship and the sacrifice that obtained in Israel was only justified, then, when it served to express this purely personal relation. When one attributed to these exercises a meaning of their own and intended thereby to supplant the relation to Jahweh with ritual acts in the Holy Place and with holy things, Baalism was perpetrated and Israel fell away from God, even though the whole thing may have proceeded in the name of Jahweh.

The withdrawal from this cultic and objectively understood worship of God is decisive in the preaching of Jesus. In it man no longer stands before God as the member of a people. He is there absolutely as the unique one. For him, in the world there are neither holy and pure things with the worship of which he could please God, nor profane and impure things abstinence from which would have the same result. Here only man himself is pure or impure, holy or profane. To use the Biblical term, these things can be said only of man's " heart." He can serve God in no other way than by " giving " him his heart. For God requires only his heart, nothing else. God desires the man himself, just as God has promised himself to man.

The God-relation is thus free of such an objective, worldly dependence. That does not mean that the man who has really entered into this relation to God is taken out of the world. For nowhere but in and toward the world which encounters him is man able to let God be his God and in this way respond to him. But he does not do this simply by distinguishing between holy and profane works. He does it, as Luther says, " not as the fools who look at their works to determine what is good or not good, thus making a distinction between the works. No, not so. Leave the works undistinguished; let one be as the other, but fear God and be righteous. Thereafter, do as you please. For even though it be doing nothing but loading manure or driving a donkey, it would be well done. Here the text is adamant: Whoever fears God will do good, though he do whatever he will." (W.A. 10, I_1, 293 f.) But if the person does good, his goodness is not a result of his works.

"Good works never change the person. Hence, even though those who wish to become holy by works do change and improve their works as they purpose to, in their person they remain as they were before. Their works become disguises for their shame and hypocrisy. But faith changes the person and makes a child of the enemy. It does this so secretly that even the outward work, position, and way of life remain unaffected unless they were by nature bad works." (W.A. 10, I_1, 228.)

The goodness of the person must precede his works. They can then be good works in the sense of the divine requirement. But they must not be understood in a simply moral sense. Therefore, as Luther says, one must rise higher in the understanding of the action than philosophy does. A completely new action must come about. Indeed, in theology as well as in philosophy the presupposition for right "action" is right insight and right will. The good tree always precedes the good fruit. In theology, moreover, the right insight and the good will is nothing but faith. (W.A. 40, I, 411.) But faith does not only bring about the good work immediately, as insight and will do in philosophy. Rather, faith brings about the good being of the person. For the good being is brought about through faith alone. This good being in which the person participates through faith is not simply moral being. For it corresponds to faith. More precisely, in this good being man corresponds to the event between God and him as he is aware of it in faith. Faith acknowledges, as we have seen, that God "has" man in mind in this event.

The meaning of God's purpose toward man we can now say is that God is good to man. In that way we express the proper meaning — the personal and the verbal character of this event. "God is good to man." When the realizing-producing thinking of subjectivism says that, it can only understand that God is *a* "good" for man, even though, of course, the "highest good" that it is man's duty to

" use." Action thus defined would still be only moral action, and its works would be of a " produced " moral quality. " God is good to man " means infinitely more. It refers, as Luther said, to the " abundant goodness of God which no prophet, no apostle, no angel, has been able to express, no heart adequately to fathom and comprehend. It is the great fire of the love of God for us by which the heart and conscience become gay, assured, and contented, that is, it is the Christian faith preached." (W.A. 10, I_1, 11.) In this abundant goodness God gives himself to man in the fullness of his deity that man may " live in the life in which God lives " (W.A. 43, 221). That is what Luther hears in the word " thy " in the First Commandment: " I am the Lord *thy* God." Just because that is what Luther heard there, he relied on this word even in the gravest temptations, as Karl Holl pointed out.

Since God gives himself to man, and with himself everything man needs, God wills that man give himself to God. For " God desires not what is ours but ourselves " (W.A. 3, 280). It is exactly the same with Christ in whom God promises himself to man. " He gives himself to me wholly and completely. He does not cut off a piece to give me. He gives the whole fountain of eternal wisdom, not a tiny trickle." "Thus Christ is to me also. He will have all of me, nothing else. And if I were to give him everything I could *do,* it would be to him as nothing. . . . Then if I am now his and he is mine, I have eternal life, righteousness, and everything that is in him." (W.A. 10, III, 416.) The good being of the person without which no good works are possible can be obtained by man in no other way than by relying on the knowledge that God is good to him. If he does that, he is in the " use " of God. Only in that way is he good. And how does he come to rely upon the knowledge that God is good to him? That can happen in no other way than in faith. As Luther says: " I believe, even if I am a sinner. For my faith should and must hold sway over everything that is and is not, sin and virtue, and everything, in order to keep oneself candidly and openly in God, as the first command urges upon me." (W.A. 7, 216.)

17. LUTHER'S WAR AGAINST FREE WILL

Luther's passionate war against "works righteousness" engaged two fronts: one was the piety of papal theology, the other was Protestant enthusiasm. While these two struggles took different forms, they were dominated by a single conviction: the relation of man to God accessible in the Christian faith decisively involves the being of God as well as the being of man. Only if that is clearly acknowledged, can one understand that it is the reality of God which is at stake and that this reality can be comprehended only by faith. For only in this way does man encounter God with his own being and thus respond to the being of God. But God's reality is his being God. That can be grasped solely by faith, by a faith in which man responds with his being to the being of God. By such faith alone can man be justified before God. As Luther's understanding of righteousness before God can be interpreted, only in such a faith does man truly respond to God and to his being God. (W.A. 40, III, 54.)

Luther had early realized that all the action of man, however constituted, misses the reality of God. None of his action makes him righteous before God because nothing he does responds to God's being. And so, as Luther says in his hymn "Out of Deep Need," "our action is in vain." Under the spell of moralistic thinking one tries to understand this line without reference to what follows in the hymn: "even in the best lives." Usually Luther is thought to mean that man is capable of ethically imperfect action only because of the Fall of man. Because of this imperfection, all his action is " in vain." One must admit that Luther's way of expressing himself does allow for such an understanding. But one should look closer, examining some of the passages that provide a background of meaning for these now debatable instances. It is not difficult to recognize in that context that it is a big mistake to interpret Luther moralistically. His thought goes much deeper. The distinction between ethically perfect and imperfect action where it is a matter of the God-relation or, as Luther says, of the justification of man makes the very mistake committed by those who would " see in works and choose on the basis of works what is good and what is not good." Luther calls these " fools." What he means by his rejection of works in relation to justification cannot be grasped in ethical categories. Something prior is presupposed. One should know that it is not simply the ethically imperfect action that is " in vain " before God. It is action in any sense.

This is the knowledge which prompted Luther to reject the doctrine of free will. It was not based in the conviction that the free will was incapable of performing morally perfect works. Luther, of course, says that man " can neither will nor do good " by the power of his will and that he can only sin, urged on by God's omnipotence (W.A. 18, 710). But one would not understand Luther if he were to conclude from such a statement that man is completely weak or devoid of any moral capacity. When Luther sees the will in the context appropriate to it he does not belittle the will. In the writing from which the above quotations have been selected, *The Bondage of the Will,* he says that " aside from the spirit, the power of the free will is the noblest power in man. For nothing higher can be said of man than that he exists in the works of the law." (W.A. 18, 765.) " Those who strive for the honest and the good with the power of the free will are the best and the most honest." (W.A. 18, 761.) The question Luther is raising about the free will, then, is not about the possibility or impossibility of a morally perfect action. It is the quite different question of whether man, by action in any sense, can achieve either something or nothing toward his salvation, whatever the quality of his works may be, even if they were to achieve the holiness of the angels (W.A. 18, 768). In the opinion of Luther, whoever lacks a clear understanding of that knows really nothing of Christian things and is worse off than the heathen (W.A. 18, 614). That is, in the matter of one's salvation, whoever "affirms the free will in the slightest degree, denies Christ" (W.A. 18, 777). For only "one who does not really doubt that he is wholly dependent on God's will, despairing completely in himself, regarding himself as nothing yet simply waiting upon the action of God, only that one is in the greatest proximity to the mercy of God and will thereby be saved." (W.A. 18, 632 f.)

Thus the decision for or against God does not have its locus in the context of action. That decision takes place prior to all action. Following upon everything we have discussed up to this point, that means that this decision occurs in faith and in no other way. What that means is understandable only if one has acknowledged that faith immediately involves the being of God. There is no greater misunderstanding of faith than to regard it as some sort of "realized" faith "in" God's being, such as the "believed" concept that there is a God. Faith is, rather, the awareness of the invisible nature of God in which man, in the nothingness of his existence as he attempts to live it on the basis of his own possibilities, experiences the nature of God, God's eternal power and deity, as his being for us. One cannot and need not speak here of a concept "of" or a faith "in." Luther rejects this in the strongest language when he says of faith that it is "entrance into the darkness in which everything man has conceived with his reason, his feeling, intellect, and understanding is consumed. For faith unites the soul with the invisible, ineffable, eternal, and unimaginable word of God and at the same time separates the soul from everything visible." (W.A. 5, 69.)

Accordingly, we can say that in faith and only in faith does the decision for God occur. For in faith man makes himself ready for the presence of God because in faith God is his God through His being-for-him. No act of "doing" can deprive faith of this decision and achieve the decision by itself. For the decision about his action is already made in the fact that a man believes or does not believe. If he has decided against God in his unbelief, all his action is sinful, the morally perfect no less than the imperfect. For the action of a man who has decided against God, Luther says, can have no other meaning than that he determines to assert himself. This pertains to actions that serve the purposes of moral righteousness as well as the actions that are carried through for the most questionable reasons. Indeed, Luther means that the free will is most evil when by use of it man strives for moral righteousness, even if in the moral sense it is the best kind of action. The more the free will strives for righteousness before God, the more evil it becomes (W.A. 18, 760). Likewise, if all the action man is capable of is sinful when it occurs in man's decision against God through his unbelief, it is clear that this decision cannot be overcome by another action, even if it were morally the most perfect conceivable. On the other hand, if a man in believing decides for God, all his action is free from sin. (W.A. 8, 89; *vere totum peccatum abolitum est, ut prorsus nihil regnet amplius.*) For in that case "the whole person is acceptable to God" (W.A. 8, 107). It would therefore be the greatest godlessness to say that whoever believes "is still in sin or that all sin is not in the fullest sense forgiven him. For what can still remain of sin where God is good to a man and determines to behold no sin, accepting and sanctifying the whole man wholly? Of course, one dare not attribute this holiness to our purity but only to the grace of God who is good to us " (W.A. 8, 107).

The meaning here becomes even clearer when one considers the distinction Luther makes between sin, on the one hand, as it is apparent to man being real in his action, and sin, on the other hand, as it condemns man, ruling over him by the law and by the wrath of God. In the former sense there is sin in the baptized and believing Christian as well. For " the incitement of anger and concupiscence lives on in the pious as well as in the impious, and he is the same before and after grace." The Spirit which makes alive (Rom. 8:2) has not yet delivered the believing man from death nor delivered him from sin. " The spirit will ultimately make him free; but now we must still die and be harassed by sin." In the sense in which the sin is condemned, however, the Spirit has already delivered the believing man from sin in that form. For " [the Spirit] has delivered him from the law of sin and death, so that sin is indeed there, but has lost its power to condemn and no longer has any authority. Death is still ahead, but it has lost its sting. It can no longer harm and terrify." (W.A. 8, 91.)

Luther lets the decision for God occur singly and alone in faith, because only in faith can man respond to the reality of God, to his being God. In this way he can indicate that the " decision " for God, which is faith, is based on the reality of God as this reality is accessible to us in God's being for us. If this decision were to take place in the action and works of man, it would be based on these actions, and would be a work of man of the same sort as all the other works of which he is capable. But if it takes place in faith, and if this faith is real faith and not merely a " believed " concept about something such as a God, then our decision is based on God's promise to us. It is based on the promise in which God has given us his very being as God and our very being as men.

Luther struggled against "works righteousness," then, because the "decision" of man is precipitated only in faith. If one knows that, he can also know that this war is at the same time a struggle for the proper freedom of man toward the world and its law. For only when this freedom is protected from delimitation can the freedom of the God-relation be protected from all self-justifying action. Now, of course, this freedom means that in the life lived for God there is no room for the law. For as soon as the law would regain its power over man, he would be living no longer for God but only for himself. No doctrine of justification, "believed" in an ever so correct theological sense, would be able to protect him from that. But the law is thoroughly valid in the life man lives in the world, including man's actions. However, because the authority of the law is abrogated with regard to the life man lives in faith, the law must be differently evaluated than if it were applicable to the life of faith as well. If the law were applicable to faith, the decision as to whether man would live to God would lie not only with faith but also with the action of man. That was the meaning of the traditional theology of Luther's times. In the same way the Roman Church considered itself the uniquely legitimate substitute for the divine power of the law on earth, the administrator of the salvation of man and the world based on the divine validity of this law, and the administrator of the power of divine grace which should make it possible for man to fulfill this law, a task considered necessary for salvation. Luther knew very exactly what a deep contradiction exists between this theology and his doctrine of faith. For his doctrine says: "If you have not died to the law, you will not live to God. Customarily it is said that if you do not live to the law, neither do you live to God. That is the opinion of all the theologians." (W.A. 40, I, 267.) But if Luther's doctrine is right, the validity of the law as it encounters man in the world and is valid here for his action is limited to the world and man's action in it.

It is true that Luther makes a sharp distinction between faith and works. It is also true that he limits the validity of the law and the works that have to be performed in the fulfillment of this law to the sphere of the world. But it is not, therefore, true that Luther belittles the meaning of these works. Indeed, conservative man that he is, he estimates very soberly the moral capacity of man, his power to do as well as his power to know, as found in the majority of people. But he is not at all of the opinion that the moral capacity, and especially the power to know, does not exist in great strength in many men. His partiality toward The Proverbs shows that. And his violent rejection of Aristotle in all theological questions has not prevented him from acknowledging Aristotle's great meaning for moral knowledge. Accordingly, he appreciates the high value of works done in obedience to the moral law, works man is quite capable of doing. Certainly man's works must conform to what he is able to accomplish by his action. That is, the works dare not be kept under the power of that " monster, the opinion of righteousness " (W.A. 40, I, 482). That is the opinion that man can realize righteousness before God by his action and with that righteousness his salvation. But if this "stubborn, rebellious beast, self-righteousness " (W.A. 40, I, 482), is deprived of its force through faith, then the world is full of possibilities for doing good works that serve life in the world. They hold the world in order. The task is given man of taking care of this order for the sake of man's and his neighbor's life in the world.

In this way an extraordinarily meaningful " transvaluation " of " good " works is achieved. " Good " is no longer the extraordinary work, chosen by man himself, fashioned after the example of the saints, and invented by man for the purpose of producing his own salvation because driven by that "*opinio iustitiae.*" If you ask those who conform to this pattern "whether they also regard it as good work when they are engaged in handicraft, or on the move, standing, eating, drinking, sleeping, and in every work near to the body or generally useful, and whether they believe that God is pleased about these works, you will find them saying no" (W.A. 6, 205). Luther, on the other hand, is of the opinion that everyone will find out what works are good "when he is aware of how God leads him and what God will have from him." And if one asks, "But if I have not been called, what shall I do?" you should answer him: "How is it possible that you have not been called? You will surely be in a calling. You are surely a married man or woman or a daughter or child, or a servant or maid. . . . See here! No one is without a command or a calling, is he? Well, no one is without works as long as he will act right." (W.A. 10, I_1, 308 f.) Those who do not understand Luther's saying that he only lives to God who dies to the law, and can think of nothing but that those who do not live to the law cannot live to God, may be compared to the curious folk in the story handed down by Aristotle. They happened to come upon Heraclitus, the great philosopher, as he was warming himself by the stove. Just as they were about to turn away disillusioned at this sight of a man chilly and exposing the whole ordinariness of his life, Heraclitus invited them to come in. "For the gods are present here too," he said. (Heidegger, *Über den Humanismus,* Frankfurt/Main, pp. 39 f.) Luther says the same thing in his own way: "What is all our work in the fields, in the garden, in the city, in the house, in fighting, in governing? Is it anything in the sight of God but the work of a child (as when little children fast and pray and spread out their clothes on Christmas Eve, that the Christ-child or St. Nicholas shall give them presents)? Will not

God give his gifts in the same way in the fields, at home, and everywhere? They are the masks of our Lord God behind which he will hide and do what he does." (W.A. 31, I, 436.)

Most important for our context in this view of the work and action of man is that Luther rejected "works righteousness" through his resolute basis in his understanding of faith. To say it positively, he kept the action of men directed to the world and to life in the world, thus safeguarding their autonomous freedom for them. This means for the world that, on the one hand, it becomes free from a law that is not appropriate to it, because its measure is distorted by the opinion of righteousness (*opinio iustitiae*) and the striving for salvation which the world can never achieve on its own basis. It means, on the other hand, that it remains open for the being of the Creator to whom it belongs as his creation. And this freedom means for the life of man in this world that he perceives the directions for his action in the reasonable knowledge of the possibilities of his life in this world. And faith is only able to fulfill its most proper task — that of safeguarding man's freedom for God — when it holds open this autonomous freedom of the world and of life in it. Only when faith does both these things is it the faith "that holds sway over everything that is and is not, sin and virtue and everything, in order to keep onself candidly and openly in God" (W.A. 7, 216).

18. THE SELF–CONSCIOUSNESS OF THE CHRISTIAN FAITH

In " keeping oneself candidly and openly in God " the self-consciousness expresses what the Christian faith makes accessible. Keeping oneself in God is " candid and open " because faith, as Luther says, " holds sway over everything that is and is not, sin as well as virtue." Luther perhaps said this even better in another statement. The believing man " must die to all things, to good and evil, to death and life, to hell and heaven, and confess from the heart that he can do nothing of his own power " (W.A. 24, 18). These statements mean that the self-consciousness of the Christian man is based in nothing that belongs to the world. For it is based in none of the possibilities that man chose in the world before the coming of faith, not even those by which he tried to obtain good, life, and heaven, or to overcome evil, death, and hell. The faith that " holds sway over everything that is and is not " precedes all such possibilities. Even though man lives in the world and lives by means of everything that exists in the world, in this faith he knows that he does not belong to the world and that he is not simply a tool as everything else existing in it is. Therefore, he understands that the knowledge of faith is not one possibility alongside other similar possibilities. Or if he does regard faith as one possibility among others, the knowledge he has is no longer knowledge of this faith. For man has the possibility of knowing himself prior to and beyond all other ways of knowledge only because he knows of the God " in whose sight" (II Cor. 2:17) alone he is the one he knows in this way. Therefore, in this knowledge he does not look upon himself as the Greek philosopher does, as "one among others." For since he knows himself in the sight of God, his angle of vision is fixed by the way God looks at him. He knows of himself in knowing that God has known him (cf. Gal. 4:9). And just as he knows himself only in this way, in faith, so he knows of God only as the One who knows him. That means that faith together with his knowledge is based on nothing that exists outside him and God, from which some kind of objective knowledge is possible. This faith is nothing, then, but faith. It is boundless. What is the same, it has no basis other than it finds in itself. Luther has innumerable statements in which he says the same thing in new formulations. "Faith beholds nothing. It is the way of darkness." (W.A. 1, 217.) "Faith has to leap from the secure bank of this life to the abyss where there is no feeling or sight, no footings or props." (W.A. 19, 217.) The darkness of this abyss is death and hell as long as man is outside it. When he ventures in faith to leap into it "without demanding information, knowledge, and security" (W.A. 5, 507 f.), then it is life and salvation (W.A. 5, 50 f.).

There are attempts to base one's faith in God and his revelation on a knowledge achieved prior to faith — which can only mean without faith — such as objective facts of salvation. Every attempt of that sort hopelessly misses God and his revelation. Every faith that does not risk acknowledging its groundlessness "believes" in something. Under some circumstances it is even a theologically "orthodox" doctrine of God. But God in his deity remains at a distance from this kind of belief. Only such a groundless faith has room for the knowledge of God which is the uniquely true knowledge of him. Faith is directed toward the "*qua re*" and not the "*quid,*" toward the "why," or the "use," of God's revelation and not toward the "what." When that is so, we can say that faith knows of God only as it allows itself to be subject to the " use " God will make of man, granting him being " in the presence of God." We have already cited Luther's bold statement about faith to the effect that this faith is the creator of the deity of God in us (though certainly not in God's person) . This statement is no bolder than the faith itself. It simply says that God is God only to the believing person. For even the fact that he wills to be God " in us," that is, to be " our " God, promising himself to us, is the " use " to which he will put us, since he pledges himself to us with his word. The selfhood man becomes aware of through the Christian faith is actually the presupposition of everything he believes. There is no other presupposition.

We have seen that Luther fought his passionate struggle against " works righteousness " for the sake of man's selfhood in the presence of God. The struggle involved obtaining autonomous freedom for the world and the life of man in it, for his action and his works. For only where this freedom is safeguarded is there room for faith and for the decision that is possible only in faith, the decision on behalf of man's filial freedom for God. Luther was conscious of the depth of the contradiction that existed between him and the whole traditional theology. For he took the decision for or against God out of the realm of man's works and attributed it to faith alone. He believed that faith can be real, pure faith only in that way. To say that faith is pure is to say it has not the least admixture of works. It believes solely on God's word. That is the word with which God promises himself to man and with his deity gives him the very life to which God calls him.

At the same time, Luther was aware that his doctrine of justification by faith alone would be exposed to the greatest danger in the future. For not only did it contradict the medieval theology which had been transmitted to Luther and against which he had to struggle. It contradicted the sectarians of his time who partially referred to him but claimed at the same time to have extended what Luther had begun, and in a more thoroughgoing way than he. His doctrine of justification by faith had to be defended on both these fronts. He acknowledged in this way that the doctrine would never be beyond attack. The form in which Luther developed his polemic with his contemporary opponents, whether Papists, enthusiasts, or Anabaptists, may be historically antiquated in more than one respect. No restoration can make Luther's doctrine what it was originally. That goes all the more for the form taken by the more or less scholastic formulations of the confessional writings of the Reformation. Little remains in them of the movement and the range for man's existence which justification by faith had originally held for Luther and which he continually maintained in such a high degree.

What Luther attempted to express in the doctrine of justification by faith, however, was conceived primarily as a polemic in the solitary discussion with himself. It pertains to the question humanity can never again avoid, now that the gospel of Jesus Christ has come into the world. And the answer must continually be found anew. That is the question as to whether one will live out of the world or out of God. Luther saw this more clearly than anyone since New Testament times. He saw that man is confronted by an inescapable alternative: he can live either out of God or out of the world. If he does the one, he cannot do the other. If he thinks he can live partly out of God and partly out of the world, he is consistent with the teaching of the Roman Church. Roman Catholicism dealt with man partly on the basis of God's mercy, partly on the basis of his merit acquired through his own piety. To live like that, however, is to live entirely out of the world, and does not do justice to God as Luther had experienced him through the Bible as it originally revealed itself to him in the solitude of his study. And yet one actually does live out of the world if one thinks he is able to live entirely out of God, as the monastic orders of the Roman Church attempted in their way, vowing to abandon the world. In another way some of the sects of the Reformation tried to live entirely out of God by withdrawing, through revolutionary force or passive resistance, from the official order and authority considered as the proper embodiment of the world. In that position one lives solely in his own tutelage, and only apparently out of the commands taken from the Scriptures. Luther realized that for the man who actually lives in the world and cannot live anywhere else there is only one possibility of living out of God and not out of the world even while living in it. That is the possibility he has called his doctrine of justification by faith alone. This doctrine presupposes a faith that is nothing but faith. Therefore, it is "held candidly and openly in God." Because of that it "holds sway over everything that is and is not, sin and virtue, and everything."

In this double characterization of faith something twofold is expressed about the self-consciousness accessible in faith. First is the situation of the self-consciousness in relation to God. This self-consciousness is so constituted, as we have seen, that man knows of himself in it only in faith, that is, in his being known of God. And he knows of God only by knowing of himself in this way. In this knowledge which is his faith, man lives entirely out of God. But that is also the description of the constitution of the self-consciousness toward the world in which man lives. It is maintained by nothing belonging to the world. Hence, man knows in this self-consciousness that he does not live *out of* the world which he nevertheless lives *in*. Nothing in the world, therefore, can separate him from God (Rom. 8:38 f.). For as surely as man lives out of God in faith he is ahead of the world. And so in this way the self-consciousness that is accessible in faith is the completely new possibility in contrast to all worldly possibilities of understanding himself. In his knowledge of God and of himself as well as in the knowledge of the world, or as Heidegger formulates it, in his " being ahead " (*Vorlaufen*), man has the " possibility of understanding the most unique, the uttermost capacity of being, that is, the possibility of an authentic existence " (Heidegger, *Sein and Zeit,* Halle/Saale, 1927, p. 263).

19. THE LOCUS OF THE DISCUSSION WITH SUBJECTIVISM

The theological discussion with modern subjectivism must begin where subjectivism has its source. The source is not where one usually looks for it. It is not to be found in modern scientific thinking, for instance. Now subjectivism is closely tied up with modern scientific thinking. But there is a difference. They are the same inasmuch as both involve man's independence toward the world and its law. Here and there, however, this independence is on a different base. The independence of modern science as it has been elaborated methodically was originally made possible by the Christian faith. For it was the Christian faith that deprived the world and its law of its religious power, surrendering to the reason the elucidation of this independence.

In modern subjectivism, then, this independence has received a completely different meaning. Subjectivism is not a matter of clearheaded, methodical, scientific research. It is, rather, a world view. It has a wholly different meaning for the independence of man, which corresponds to it. Subjectivism has become a world view which claims to be valid for everything there is. That is consistent with what we have recognized concerning the source of subjectivism.

Not the least of the reasons for its origin lies in the necessity modern science has seen for defending its freedom in the face of the claims of church doctrine. (Compare what Heidegger says about the source of the subjectivistic " claim of man to a *fundamentum absolutum inconcussum veritatis* ": " Why and how does this claim achieve such decisive respect? The claim originates from the liberation of man in which he frees himself from the bondage of the truth of the Christian revelation and of church doctrine and makes himself his own lawgiver. Through this liberation the essence of freedom is newly posited as a bondage to what is binding. But because the man liberating himself determines what shall be binding according to this freedom, hereafter the freedom becomes variously determined. The source of the bondage can be the human reason and its law, or it can be the existence of something not oriented to and objectively ordered by the reason, the chaos not yet ordered by the objectification and first calling for mastery in any age." *Holzwege,* pp. 98 f.)

As we have seen, this conflict is based in the fact that, in spite of Luther, faith was no longer understood by the church and its theologians as a justifying faith in the full sense. In consequence, it no longer had the freedom toward the world and its law that it possessed for Paul and that Luther again brought to light. And when science in the autonomy of its task and responsibility began to elaborate man's independence toward the world in a way suitable to itself, the conviction arose that the church should restrict the freedom of science in the name of faith. On the other hand, scientific thinking began to assert its freedom, since it posited reason in the place of faith. With the help of reason and in its name, science carried out its task in autonomous responsibility. That means, as we have seen, that in modern subjectivism and in the scientific thinking dominated by it, man has undergone a change. In the Christian faith he is understood as a created being.

In modern subjectivism he can understand himself only as being the source of meaning for all existence. The meaning of the independence of man, therefore, has undergone a radical change. In faith it is an independence in which man knows himself " out of God in the presence of God," since he knows that God knows him and in this independence man is the presupposition of all he believes. In modern science independence has shifted to something that is based in itself and in the nature of man as a rational animal.

The discussion with modern subjectivism must proceed at this level, then, where it has its source. It follows that faith must again be acknowledged in the full sense as that which alone justifies, the sense in which Paul and then Luther had understood and taught it. But that cannot come about simply by reconstructing this understanding historically (*historisch*). That procedure would make sense only if we could make the original historical situation our own. But the spiritual situation of the apostle Paul and of Luther is no longer our situation. Indeed, it is through their faith that our quite different spiritual situation has come into existence. Hence, the problem that is put to faith in the modern world is a problem of its own creation. The problems Luther faced already represented a considerable modification of the problems faced by the apostle Paul. In distinction from both, however, through modern science the independence of man toward the world and its law has been realized to an extent never before known in the history of the Christian faith. That this could happen at all lay in the faith and its denial of the religious power of the world and its law.

Now the task of understanding the faith in the last analysis is still the same. One must understand it in such a way as to safeguard the freedom of man for God. Today as always that is possible only if faith is understood in such a way as to provide a sphere for the freedom and independence of man toward the world and its law. But let us first attempt to clarify the distinction between our situation and Paul's. For Paul the world toward which faith made freedom accesible was the world of the classical man. Where Paul speaks of the victory of faith over the world, the adversary that is overcome is referred to as the principalities and powers of the cosmos (e.g., Rom. 8:38 f.). The power and right with which these forces have held man captive to their religious authority is overthrown because faith has recognized their creatureliness. Paul did not deny their reality. In another place he expressly concedes that there are actually " many 'gods' and many 'lords,' in heaven and on earth." But they are only " so-called " gods. " By nature " they are " no gods." But compared with the " one God, the Father, from whom are all things and for whom we exist, and one Lord, Jesus Christ, through whom are all things and through whom we exist," they are " weak and beggarly elemental spirits." (I Cor. 8:5 f. and Gal. 4:8 f.; also compare I Cor. 10:18 ff.)

For us the whole thing is basically different. Hence, we cannot simply repeat what the apostle has said about the victory of faith in the same sense and with the same images he has employed without doing something more. For his world is no longer our world. Indeed, our world is as Paul's, overcome by powers of law, as we have already seen. But these laws are completely different from the laws Paul had to cope with. The world of the apostle and his contemporaries attributed to the law a religious authority giving it a mysterious power over man, so that even though " by nature " it was " no god," they were required to serve it in religious worship (Gal. 4:8). Now, however, the opposite is the case. The lawfulness of natural and historical powers, which science rationally investigates and which powerfully penetrate the world, has become the means through which man obtains ever greater dominance over the world and becomes increasingly independent toward it.

He could do so because faith gave him the possibility of distinguishing between the law " of the Spirit which makes alive " and the law " of sin and death " (ch. 8:2), or, as he also says, between the " new Spirit " and the " old letter " (ch. 7:6). He has combined what he has to say about this fate in two sentences: " So I find it to be a law that when I want to do right, evil lies close at hand. For I delight in the law of God, in my inmost self, but I see in my members another law at war with the law of my mind and making me captive to the law of sin which dwells in my members." (Ch. 7:21 ff.) These sentences, heavy in content and difficult to understand, should be understood as follows: The law appears in these sentences in three forms that are profoundly distinguishable from each other. The " law of God," to which the inward man cheerfully consents, and " the law of my mind " are one and the same form. Hence, the inner " man " and the " mind " mean man in the same aspect, that is, as the one " who wants to do the good " and who agrees " that the law is good " (vs. 16 and 19). In distinction to this, the other two expressions about the law do not mean the same thing. " The law in my members " is not the same as " the law of sin which dwells in my members," even though in both instances it is said of the law that it is " in my members." For it is said of the former that it brings me into captivity to the latter. These expressions would have no meaning if in both instances the same form were intended.

To understand this statement one must understand what is meant by the word " member," for that is the locus of both forms of the law. A glance at the context of this sentence makes it clear that when the " members " of man are referred to, the expression has to do with his action. But in this passage the action of man appears as something " evil " in opposition to his " will " which is good (v. 19). One must therefore be on guard against the inference that " action " as such is sinful. Action is no more sinful than the " member " as such is sinful. In ch. 6, Paul makes the point that the " member " can be used as well for the service of lawlessness as for the service of righteousness (v. 19). When the law " in my members " is referred to here as warring against the law of " my mind," it must be realized that this does not mean " the law in my members " as such. If one fails to realize this, it is impossible to understand what Paul wishes to say by way of both expressions.

Finally, we must still ask what kind of law it is that Paul calls the law " of sin which dwells in my members " and what kind of law it is according to which when I would do the good I can do nothing but evil. We remember that Paul speaks in this passage of a deception of sin. The entanglement of truth and error has been accomplished by this deception and cannot be unraveled. That is what ch. 7:11 means: " For sin, finding opportunity in the law [that is, as it is already expressed in v. 8, " wrought in me all kinds of covetousness "], deceived me and by it killed me." (The Greek word *entole* does not mean here simply the single command but the law as a whole; compare W. Bauer, *Wörterbuch zum Neuen Testament.*) It is impossible to grasp the meaning of this expression if " covetousness," which is wrought by sin with the help of the law, is taken to mean only something sensual. This, of course, can be a part of the meaning in so far as it is also a part of life. But in the proper sense the " covetousness " awakened by sin is any " zeal for God " (Rom. 10:2) that, because it is awakened through sin, no longer acknowledges God in the right way. If this " zeal for God " has been awakened by the law under the influence of sin — and for Paul that means the exchanging of the Creator for the creature — and if it appeals to the law, then it " did not see fit to acknowledge God " as it had originally (ch. 1:28 and 32). In that case it contains a meaning hostile to God (which is what Paul calls "covetousness") and urges man to seek to establish his own righteousness as the

Jews did on the basis of their own works, orienting their piety to the law, hence, without a right knowledge of God and his righteousness (ch. 10:3). In other words, the " zeal " for God is awakened through the law. In that case the zeal really no longer has God as its purpose but man, and the law becomes the means of justifying man and thus achieving his life. In this way, however, the law brings man inescapably under the domination of sin and death. For not only is " the zeal for God " transmuted into " covetousness," but the law also is perverted into the law " of sin and death." Or, what is the same, the law becomes religiously worshiped. (Compare what was said earlier about the law weakened by " the flesh.")

" Covetousness " understood in this way for the first time brings about the character of fate. For since it appeals to the law, in this the inextricable entanglement of error and truth originates which, in its inability to be disentangled, expresses the nature of fate. Sin can awaken covetousness with the help of the law because it has its basis in the fact that " the inner man " consents to the law, for he knows that the law is good and that it is given him for the sake of life. Hence, the " law in my members " is useful in this deception because it calls man to action. But what is the deception by which sin deludes man? According to Paul, the first result is that the law, used by sin, brings man death and not life, as man expected. Because he expects life he consents to the law and, to say the same, performs the works corresponding to it. Man himself, therefore, bears " fruit for death " (ch. 7:5). Together with what he does according to the law, man is the prey to " nothingness," instead of doing as he " would " when he followed the law, namely, bear fruit for God, thus obeying God and having his life in that obedience. But how can this deception exist without man's knowing it? Where is the original fault, the *proton pseudos* from which everything else follows of necessity? Now, this *proton pseudos* is sin itself. We recall the sin Paul speaks about. It is exchanging the Creator for the creature. This " exchanging " is not simply something one has done at one time that he can treat as if he had not done it or perhaps even overcome. For what has happened concerns the Creator and the creature, hence, the original order of being. The destiny of a perversion of being occurs in it, therefore, which precedes all doing of " this or that " but also effects all action that follows, so that it happens inevitably within this perversion. And when Paul lets the man he mentions here say, " I am carnal, sold under sin " (v. 14: the image that is used in this expression as a metaphor is that of a slave brought under the authority of a lord by sale), what he means by it is just a destinating event.

The profoundest forcefulness of this destiny first appears when one acknowledges that the law under which man stands is drawn along in this perversion. For since this perversion happens to the law, one can say that destiny as such is irrevocably fixed. Nothing that occurs in this sphere — and everything belongs to it that is subject to the law, hence, the entire human existence — can extricate itself from it. That is what Paul means when he says in v. 18, " I can will what is right, but I cannot do it." One should not try to understand this sentence in moral terms any more than he would anything else Paul says in this chapter. Thus he will not say that the man he speaks of here, although he has the right moral knowledge, lacks the moral power to realize this knowledge in his action. Paul speaks, rather, of a destiny under which this man stands and by which his whole being is determined, whether or not he knows it. The immediately preceding sentence indicates that clearly enough. It says of this man that in him, that is, in his " flesh," dwells no good thing. But that repeats the earlier sentence to the effect that man is " sold under sin," that he thus stands under this destiny of the perversion of sin. (Compare what was said above about the "flesh" and the "nothingness of the world.") But that means that even the good that this man wills, when he does it, is subjected to this perversion, and hence is not the "good he would." That is why this man does not understand his own action — as Paul has interpreted the fallen existence under this destiny. For he does not do what he wills but does what he hates. He does the opposite of what he would do. Here in this exchange, which man himself accomplishes without being able to know it as such, is the *proton pseudos*.

Sin also deceives man in that under its dominion he does evil when he would do the good. That is why Paul can say in v. 20 that it is not actually man who acts here but sin. For what man does here is done under the power of sin which is the power that destiny has as the perversion of being, the exchanging of the Creator for the creature. This exchange is covered over and therefore unrecognizable for man, yet at the same time it becomes a destiny man cannot overcome, since the worship of the creature in place of God the Creator resulting from that exchange is accomplished in the name of the law and hence in the name of God. This is what is meant in that obscure, enigmatic statement of the apostle that the "law in my members" brings me into captivity to "the law of sin in my members." As we said, the "law in my members" is the law as it refers to man in regard to his action. Sin with the help of this law awakens "covetousness" to do the works that this law demands for righteousness before God. When it does so, sin uses the good for that purpose, that is, the law that is "holy, right, and good" and man's consent to it. But when man is destined to fulfill the law under the power of the perversion of being that is brought about by sin, from this "law in my members" proceeds the "law of sin which dwells in my members." And this is the fate that inescapably comes over man when he thinks he should be able to become righteous by his own works. This same fate is meant in the sentence, " So I find it to be a law that when I want to do right, evil lies close at hand " (v. 21). Now Paul did overcome the fate in which the law had imprisoned the pre-Christian man, Jews as well as Greeks (ch. 3:9). That he did so was possible only because in faith in the crucified and risen Christ he gained the knowledge of man's existence as he can live it in the freedom for God, which is accessible in faith. That is the existence as it is granted him solely out of the eternal power and deity of God. He makes the dead live and calls the nonexistent into being. He also lets man be manifested in his presence as the one who is fallen into death and vanity. Such an existence is beyond fate. What brought this fate about can no longer occur in this existence. That is, as Paul has said it, sin awakens covetousness in man through the law and deceives one who seeks life in the law. For it subjects him through the law to its own domination and the domination of death (chs. 7; 8; and 11). In this faith Paul was able to think the existence of man as it belongs to him in the double freedom, the freedom of the son for God and the freedom of the heir toward the world, and as it is delivered as such from the fate of the perverted law.

Earlier we made it clear that the unique task of faith is to safeguard this double freedom of the son and heir. We also acknowledged that faith can fulfill this task only if it has the power to grant man freedom from the law. It receives this power from the freedom for God, which is accessible in faith. For, to say it negatively, the law and, with it, the world lose their religious authority through faith; hence, they cease to be the way to the salvation of man and the world, as they were before faith entered. To say it positively, freedom from the law means that the knowledge of the law and the decision about the works that the law demands are surrendered by faith to the reason as its responsibility. If faith can give man freedom from the law in this double sense, that is a certain sign that it is really faith, that it is the faith that alone justifies, the faith in which the freedom of the son for God and of the heir toward the world is made accessible. Paul proclaimed this solely justifying faith with the gospel of the crucified and risen Christ, that all who believe, Jews and Greeks alike, may have the power of God unto salvation. That is why he could take the power from the destiny of the perversion of being which was brought about by sin, and put the right question about the fate that had kept the pre-Christian man in captivity to the law.

20. MODERN MAN'S RESPONSIBILITY FOR HIS WORLD

The situation of the apostle Paul is no longer our situation. It is like ours, however, in one important respect. The decisive thing for us as for him is to understand faith as that which alone justifies and to understand the task of faith as that of guarding the freedom of God accessible in it. But compared with New Testament times, our time is different in the respect that it is no longer the worship of the cosmic powers which threatens this freedom. Something like a religious worship absolutely cannot be given to a world toward which man has realized his autonomy in the degree and in the kind that modern man has in relation to his world. The decisive thing is that modern man is no longer responsible to the world and its power as the classical man and, in a modified way, even the medieval man was. Instead, he has become the one who is responsible *for* his world. This is so exactly to the extent and in the way in which he has become independent toward it.

Modern man owes this independence to his science. For

through it the religiously worshiped power of the world has been turned into forces the lawful functioning of which is investigated by science in ever higher degree and which man can accordingly press into his service. In doing that, man assumes responsibility for the world, for its being and remaining a world. In this responsibility the law gains power over him in a wholly new way. He cannot extricate himself from it. We have remembered the world view tendencies in ideologies and utopias, so characteristic for modern thought, which contain an especially clear expression of this power. Now, it has been the nature of subjectivism to imagine man as the one being " upon whom all being in its way of being and in its truth is based." Further, it assumes that therewith " the kind of human being originates who occupies the sphere of human capacity as the locus of the standard and the achievement for the mastery of being " (Heidegger, *Holzwege,* pp. 81 and 84). It then becomes understandable that the responsibility for the world as conceived under the constraint of subjectivism knows no other foundation and can know no other than the one given in man as he understands himself as the " sub-ject " who, " present as foundation, assembles everything around himself " (*ibid.,* p. 81).

As for the responsibility of modern man for his world, it is not difficult to see that it embraces the whole of the world as it does the responsibility. It is the responsibility accessible in the freedom of man for God that is safeguarded by faith. Hence, there appears to be a real similarity between faith and modern science. But actually there is the profoundest difference. This is most clearly seen when one considers what the notion of " the whole of the world " means for the responsibility of faith and for modern responsibility, respectively. In the responsibility of faith the whole of the world means the whole as it is constituted in being God's creation. It can be safeguarded by man only if in faith, as the mature son in the world granted him as heir, he is aware of the presence of God the Creator enduring in it as the inheritance. This faith would not be the faith that constitutes the freedom of the son for God if it did not at the same time surrender the world to man and his reason as a possession that man has to administer independently. What man does in the world toward which he is independent (what Paul calls "works") can never, therefore, mean that the wholeness of the world has somehow to be constituted by these works. If man would do what he does as "works," in this intention he would act against faith and deny the wholeness of the world. For the world's wholeness rests upon the eternal power and deity of God, as further revealed in the sending of Jesus Christ.

The concept of the whole of the world has an entirely different meaning in the responsibility that is developed for modern man through his science. In the process of modern science man has not primarily attempted to assume responsibility for the whole of the world. In all its forms science has had its origin in the elementary impulse of man to knowledge. Knowledge in the Western sense first arose with the Greeks, since they subjected science to the rule of logic and method in order not simply to "mean" but to "know" dependably. And what we call modern science arose primarily with the beginning of modern times. For only then did science become free of the limits imposed by the classical concept of the world. These limits remained in force throughout the entire Middle Ages by virtue of the hierarchical-sacramental domination of the church and its theology over the world and ultimately over the whole spiritual life. Until then this concept of the world as closed in itself preserved for science the character it had already had for the Greeks. As Karl Jaspers has said of Greek science, it could only move "within what was finished." Thus conceived, there is in ancient Greek science "neither the universal will to knowledge nor the bursting force of the will to truth." (Karl Jaspers, *Vom Ursprung und Ziel der Geschichte,* München, 1940, p. 112.)

These, however, are the attributes of modern science. Its questioning is unlimited. It is directed to everything man encounters. In its research it is never finished with even a single phenomenon. "It is dominated by a consciousness of the hypothetical, that is, by a consciousness of the presuppositions from which one proceeds continually. Everything is there to be overcome (for the presuppositions are grounded and relativized by more comprehensive presuppositions). Or if there are facts, they are there to be developed in the continuity of increasing and more deeply penetrating knowledge." (*Ibid.*) In the limitlessness of this interrogation, science is directed to the whole of the world. But as long as it questions methodically, that is, as long as it goes from question to question, it knows that it will never embrace the whole of the world. In spite of its fragmentary character, the knowledge of science gives man power over what he knows, just because it is methodical. But where there is power, responsibility develops for that over which one has power. Here is the point at which a most important decision must be made, perhaps the most important there is for the man of today.

Let us remember what we made clear earlier in relation to faith. The point about which we are speaking is the point at which faith says, "All things are permitted, but not all things are helpful." This is the point at which faith, by the power of the freedom for God safeguarded by it and accessible in it, opens to man at one and the same time freedom for himself and independence toward the world. But this independence, although originally accessible by faith, is still a fact of the reason. Hence, it must be elaborated by this reason. We have already seen that this elaboration has happened in the course of time in very different degrees.

With Paul, who was the first to treat the problem explicitly, the elaboration occurred to a relatively slight extent, so great and comprehensive is the basic meaning of his knowledge. This knowledge concerns the freedom toward the law religiously worshiped until then. In regard to the Jews, the law Paul has in mind is the traditional law on which they rely and by virtue of which they boast of their piety (Rom. 2:17). In regard to the " pagan " the law is the bondage through the cult to " gods many and lords many " which are nevertheless " by nature " no gods. Independence is achieved in this freedom in relation to the " works " man should do " in the body " as his own deeds (II Cor. 5:10). That concerns the question as to whether or not a man should eat meat offered to idols. Regarding such works, Paul requires his reader to conduct an examination and decide for himself what he is commanded to do. The test of this independence as well as its character is expressed in the fact that man no longer is responsible *before* the world and its law, as he was in the pre-Christian times. He is rather responsible *for* the world and its law. In virtue of that, the religious power of the world and its law is ended. Therefore, when one became a Christian in this early time, it was clear to him that to worship the world and its law religiously, as he had up until then, had become impossible for him. But what if he still expected his salvation in some sense from the world, either as Jew or as " pagan "? What if he expected it from the powers of the law permeating the world in its height and depth, its present and future, and so determining life and death? (Rom. 8:38.) If he did, Christ would have died in vain for him and would have been of no advantage to him. (Gal. 2:21 and ch. 5:2.) This loss of religious power concerns the law primarily in its cultic particulars, while the moral command remains valid. In that distinction, an odd reduction of the law had its beginning. This concerns not only the ritual commands, however, but the moral commands as well, although in a different way. It concerns the moral commands in so far as they lose the lawfully justifying power they had when they formed a unity with the ritual commands. Hence, man attains an independence toward them in which he is challenged to prove them. As we have already seen, Paul finds this moral command in the traditional morality as it encountered the Jews in the Old Testament, particularly in the Decalogue (Rom. 2:21 f.; 13:8-10; Gal. 5:14) and as it witnessed to the "heathen" in his conscience (Rom. 2:14 f.).

With Luther this independence toward the world and its law is elaborated much more broadly. It concerns the whole life of the world and its orders. Thus Luther gives to the whole sphere, which he calls the "worldly positions" (*Stände*), its independence to be regulated by the reason. For him even the position of the "preacher" belongs to the world. The fact that he says every Christian is in the spiritual position on the basis of his faith indicates in what an all-embracing way he understands the autonomous sphere of life in the world. But the consequence is that the reduction of the law that began with Paul progresses in a decisive way with him. Nevertheless, one must distinguish here between the law as it is valid for life in the world and its orders, and its uniquely moral character, that is, the demand of the law as it is intended for man himself in his innermost existence. Indeed, there are already in Luther's thought the beginnings of a historical understanding of the form of the human orders of life. Yet the social and political order valid for his time and the commands corresponding to it are in general still those which are given once for all in human nature and therefore the only possible ones.

This view which still belonged to the Middle Ages disappeared more and more in the course of modern times. In its place there appeared another that is one of the characteristics of the independence of man toward the world developed since the beginning of modern times. This change was made possible through modern science. Indeed, this is so because science unfolded not only as a science of nature but as a science of history as well. Through the discovery and exploration of the powers of nature, the science of nature made it possible with the help of technology for these forces, methodically used, to be inserted in higher and higher degree into human life and its formation. On the other side, the research of history acknowledged the almost unlimited metamorphosis of the historical orders of human life in state and society. Scarcely any of the forms that once existed and that will yet develop can claim for themselves an absolute validity. Luther still thought in medieval terms when he made claims for the dominant political and social order of his time. But he did not think at all in medieval terms with relation to the moral character of the demand of the law. As he understands it, man is challenged by the demand of the law as an individual and with his whole being. With him it is not a matter of " this or that " command as it appears alongside others in the written law. Hence, it is not a matter of " this or that " work demanded once for all, but of the *person* of man. Man should be good. But he will not become good through works. The works will be good through him. For " the will inwardly is the weight of all outer works and life." (W.A. 1, 163.) Here, then, man is called to himself in the most significant way. " We are all called to death together, and no one can die for another. Each must shift for himself at the time of death: for I will not be with you, nor you with me." (W.A. 10, III, 1.) Luther customarily speaks in this way of the law only when he wishes to clarify how its demand looks when taken as the demand of God, when, as he once expressed it, man has not only the commands (*mandata*) of the law to deal with but also the commanding God (*deus mandans*). (W.A. 4, 305.) This meaning of the command put to man was first accessible to faith. Luther came to understand it as he learned to understand the preaching of the Bible in its twofold sense as law and gospel. But when this understanding of moral demand is once disclosed, reason cannot avoid it.

With Luther it was still the knowledge of faith that allowed him to say, " God wants our good works to be our own and not the works of the taskmaster, the law, death, or of hell and heaven " (W.A. 10, I_1, 453). With Kant, however, it is the moral reason that let him say, " There is nothing thinkable in the world, yea, even outside it, that could be taken for good without limitation, except the good will." That means a will that is good " not through what it does or purposes, not through its fitness for achieving some purposed end, but only through the fact that it is good in itself." As Kant continues to say, even if nothing were done by the will and there were remaining " only the good will (of course, not simply as a mere wish but as the straining of all means in our power), it would be like a jewel shining for itself, which has its complete value in itself. Usefulness or fruitlessness can neither add nor subtract from this value." (*Werke,* Cassirer Ausgabe, Vol. 4, p. 250.) This knowledge of morality which Kant has formulated most clearly was further developed by his successors in a way that cannot be surrendered. The law as a sum of demands valid once and for all has been reduced to the responsibility of man for his world and for its being and remaining a world. This is a responsibility that has continually to be achieved anew as well as perceived anew. (Compare in my book *Der Mensch zwischen Gott und Welt,* 2d edition, pp. 190 ff., the section entitled " Das Ethos des neuzeitlichen Menschen.")

The change that has taken place in man's relation to the world since the beginning of modern times is a profound one. One who has not realized that and continues to live with the image of a world enclosing man by an eternal order that is valid once for all will necessarily regard it as a mistake to reduce the law to the responsibility of man. He will blame it for the peculiar uncertainty in all moral questions which has become an increasingly great care to modern man. He would be of the opinion that this uncertainty could be removed by finding a law that would be valid once and for all and binding on man in all his action. He might find such a law in some new form of the so-called "natural law." Nevertheless, if one has realized the change of his relation to the world in its entirety, such an idea must be regarded as an evasion of the task put to modern man along with his independence toward the world. Nothing that belongs to his world can be exempted from the responsibility accessible to man in this way. For the man for whom this changed relation to the world has become valid there can be nothing further that can restrict him in the sense in which the pre-Christian, mythical world did. A "natural law," however, would be such a restriction *before* which he would have to be responsible. Certainly the question that was and will be the most important for men of all times is the question about "what should be and what always is." But for modern man that can no longer be the Platonic question "about the permanent archetype of things" (Gerhard Krüger, *Die Geschichte im Denken der Gegenwart,* Frankfurt/M., p. 34). For modern man what should be and ever is can be nothing but the responsibility that he has for the being and continuing of his world. These things I have been saying about responsibility have nothing in common with responsibility as it has come to be understood under the rule of modern subjectivism.

We have already expressed the surmise that it is the responsibility understood in this way that imprisons modern man in its bonds with the inextricability of a fate, just as the law did in the form it took with the pre-Christian man. If that is so, everything depends on whether we can achieve an understanding of faith that helps us uncover in the responsibility modern man cannot escape such an inextricable and fateful entanglement of error and truth as Paul uncovered in the pre-Christian form of the law and overcame through his understanding of faith. In the light of everything we have acknowledged up to now, the new understanding cannot be achieved by changing something in the faith. On the contrary, the task before us is to regain the understanding of faith as it is witnessed to in the New Testament. But that is certainly impossible if we surrender our own historical situation. It is even less possible because, as we have tried to show, this situation has become fundamentally different from the situation of the New Testament just by virtue of the historical efficacy of faith. We must seek to gain this new understanding of faith to a greater extent in the express discussion with our present situation, meaning discussion with the subjectivism that dominates our thinking. In our effort to understand the faith given in the New Testament, we have oriented ourselves chiefly to the theology of Paul. We have done so for the reason that Paul as none of the other theologians of the New Testament has reflected the peculiar problems that characterize the understanding of faith. From Paul we have learned that the essence of the Christian faith is that faith alone justifies. Therefore, in faith the freedom of man for God is accessible as well as his independence toward the world and its law. Faith conserves both these freedoms.

The few indications we have given concerning the independence of modern man toward his world may already show in what degree modern man has become independent, a degree never attained in the history known to us. That goes not only for the scientists and technologists participating in the establishment of this independence but for everyone living in this world. Only a few are accomplishing what we have called the elaboration of this independence. Yet we are all entitled to it and as our self-evident right we can exercise it to a greater or less extent daily and hourly. To embrace it is to embrace the responsibility that accompanies it. Even when we are not conscious of it, we experience its weight in one way or another. Whoever becomes aware of this weight as the responsibility imposed on him as on all others, also knows it is rightfully imposed on him and that he cannot escape it.

That is what was meant by the assertion that the responsibility for his world is the form in which the law exercises its power over modern man. The form is changed as man's relation to the world changes. I have also said in this connection that the burden of this more or less consciously felt responsibility is not at last the reason that modern scientific thinking, contrary to its own nature, has so easily succumbed to the temptation of subjectivism as a world view.

21. THE FATE OF RESPONSIBILITY

One question still remains. Does our surmise prove true? The law exercises dominion over modern man in the form of responsibility. Is there actually a fate accompanying the dominion of the law that is similar to the fate Paul once brought to light which he overcame with the help of faith? Or is this way of thinking perhaps only an error? As pious men often believe today, is it something one could get at, such as what might be called the pride of modern man? Has man simply presumed proudly upon his responsibility, so that he ought to give it back again to God? God is the Creator and Lord of the world. Why not simply trust that he will make everything right again? For "he is wonderful in counsel, and excellent in wisdom"! (Isa. 28:29.)

Certainly either of these attitudes is right. But what of the person on whom this responsibility has once been imposed in the daily reality of his life and who therefore knows what it could mean for him and his world if he were to decline the responsibility? It would not help him very much if nothing more than this could be said. Nor did Paul believe he could conquer the fate of the law with a wave of the hand by declaring the law to be sin (although he came near to doing so; cf. Rom. 7:7). However, neither do we arrive at the fate that is hidden in this responsibility by calling it the pride of modern man, although this suggestion is not completely false. But if we meant it seriously and had said everything about this responsibility there is to say, it and everything affiliated with it in the contemporary world would be nothing but a horrible mistake.

Before one seriously claims that responsibility in the modern world is nothing but error and pride, one must concede that even though the supposed error has many threatening results, it makes life possible for innumerable men in the world today. Yet we have seen that the responsibility for the world has its source in the Christian faith. It is bound up with the Christian faith in a double way. First, only faith can fulfill it. For faith safeguards the world as the divine inheritance through which God has granted man nothing less than the possibility of filial freedom for him. Along with this freedom God has given the "awareness" (*Wahrnehmung*) of the lasting (*währenden*) presence of God's fatherhood and creatorhood in the world, and at last with this awareness, the justification uniquely suited to man. Secondly, the responsibility is bound up with faith in the sense that faith has made man responsible for the independent, rational fulfillment of responsibility through his works. Over responsibility, therefore, there stands the great word of promise, "All things are yours" (I Cor. 3:21). In this light one will have to think about whether what can be said of this responsibility may not be the same as what Paul has said of the law. Paul called the law "holy and just and good" (Rom. 7:12). But he said that of the same law he had just said proved to be a means of death to man (v. 10).

By determining that the law is holy, just, and good, Paul averts the notion that the law as such, which is good and given man for life, has become death for him. He infers that it is sin, instead, that has fraudulently brought death to man through the good, through the law. By virtue of that fraudulence sin has become effective in its exceeding sinfulness (v. 13). Now if we are right in asserting that the responsibility for the world is the form in which the law encounters modern man, then it would not be the responsibility as such that "works death" in man. Rather, it would be the sin that exploits the responsibility as a means to death. Sin "awakens" in the responsibility of man the zeal to fulfill the responsibility. That is the very thing that happened with the law. Both the responsibility and the zeal to fulfill it undergo a basic change. The basis is no longer God but man.

Let us remind ourselves that the responsibility of man for the world, for its being and remaining the world as it is originally accessible in the Christian faith, concerns the world as a whole. It concerns the world in its being and remaining whole, and that means in its being and remaining as it is by the creatorhood of God. Only faith can fulfill the responsibility for this, and even then it can do so only if at the same time it surrenders to reason the autonomous responsibility for what man is given to do in the world. Now the same thing happens to this responsibility that Paul said has happened to the law. The "zeal" to fulfill it is awakened through sin. Although that is essentially the same thing that happens to the law, it looks very different. The reason is that the situation the contemporary man finds himself in respecting the " law " is basically quite different from the situation of the apostle Paul and his congregations. For the situation in Paul's time resulted from sin, from the exchange of the Creator with the creature, necessitating the religious worship of the world and its law. That is no longer the case for the man of today. We have shown the reasons. They can be summarized in the assertion that, for us, responsibility for the world has taken the place of the religious worship of the world and its law. Man can no longer worship what he is responsible for.

Now if it is sin that, with the help of responsibility, awakens in man the " zeal " to fulfill this responsibility, both the responsibility and the " zeal " are basically changed. Their basis is no longer God but man. Furthermore, the " sin " of modern man is also that he has worshiped a creature instead of God. According to Luther's interpretation of the First Commandment in his Greater Catechism, to worship something as one's God means that " one looks to it for all good and takes refuge in it for all his needs; thus to have a God is nothing else than to trust him and believe on him from the heart, as I have often said, that only the trusting and the believing of the heart makes for both a God and an idol " (W.A. 30, I, 133). Thus for the modern man the creature, worshiped instead of God, can no longer refer to the religiously worshiped world and its law. For him the creature to which he " looks for all good and seeks refuge in all his need " is himself. Indeed, as we can now say, the creature who has supplanted the Creator is man — man as he understands himself under the domination of modern subjectivism, man the " measure and basis " of all being. Hence, the " law " through which he can know himself bound in an ultimate sense, embracing his whole existence, is no longer the law of the world. It is the responsibility as he is aware of it, with his reason on the basis of the independence toward the world that this reason elaborates. It is the responsibility as he knows himself responsible for the world according to his independence.

Of course the modern man can evade his responsibility. Instead of assuming the seriousness and the burden of the responsibility laid on him with the independence toward his world, in the arbitrariness under which his thinking then necessarily falls he can choose something that is in his world as that from which he expects a great deal, as a point of purchase. This actually happens in numberless ways with more or less seriousness. But such symbols from religions or world view have hardly anything to do with the actual situation of the contemporary man, or, if they do, then mostly only with more or less chance manifestations. So they remain stuck in the subjectivistic arbitrariness by which they are chosen. The binding relation to history and its reality out of which all the seriousness of genuine decision can develop is missing in them. Unfortunately the proclamation of the Christian faith in the church only too often proceeds in just such an estrangement from the historical reality of the contemporary world, so that even the decision for the Christian faith appears with many men to be made in mere subjectivistic arbitrariness. The feeling for the criterion of the genuineness of the faith has not become lost for the last time through that fact. Therefore, one must be ready to be engaged with seriousness and severity without which something like the responsibility for the world, which is laid upon modern man, cannot be given.

It is no longer true of this responsibility that it can be fulfilled only by faith, however. For it is indeed basically different from the responsibility before God, whose foundation can only be the creative speech of God. With that speech God calls what is not into being, and man can respond to that call only by faith. Out of this responsibility another responsibility has now been created that has its foundation in man rather than in God. Man believes he must now fulfill this responsibility by his own works. Moreover the " zeal " to responsibility is no longer of a kind that recognizes no other end than God, " by whom, in the sight of whom " (II Cor. 2:17) alone is man genuinely responsible. Out of this " zeal " for God, " covetousness " develops in man to fulfill the responsibility for the world with works and so to justify himself in his independence toward the world. His knowledge of the powers of the world and his dominion over them has made this effort possible.

It seems to me there is no doubt that in this responsibility, even though it is in a considerably changed situation, the same fateful entanglement of error and truth has occurred as dominated Paul and his time before the coming of faith. I mean, the situation is such that man cannot extricate himself from it. With Paul it was the law that had become the fate. That is, without ceasing to be the law obligating one in the name of God, it became a curse to those who tried to fulfill it through their works (Gal. 3:10) . Sin took possession of the law and by it aroused in man " covetousness " for his " own righteousness " (Rom. 10:3) . Thus the law, to which man consented because it was given to him for the sake of life, became " the power of sin " and of death (I Cor. 15:56) . In the same way the responsibility by which man originally responded to the Fatherly promise that called him into being has become for us the responsibility in which man withholds himself from God. For in that responsibility there is something from which he cannot withdraw because his being as a man is at stake. Yet " covetousness " is awakened to realize through his works the wholeness and health of his world without which it cannot be truly a world to him.

The confusion in the entanglement of error and truth that comes into dominance here is extensive. It can first become completely clear when one acknowledges that it is the faith itself through which the responsibility for man's world becomes accessible in its twofold sense. On the one side, there is the responsibility that can be fulfilled only by faith in the " awareness " of the lasting presence of God's creatorhood and fatherhood in the world. On the other side, there is the responsibility that is granted to man to be carried out by the autonomous decisions of his reason. However, precisely with this acknowledgment the possibility is also given of unraveling this entanglement of error and truth. For with it the fate holding sway there can be laid hold upon.

Paul was also able to do this in relation to the law only because he achieved in faith an understanding of the law that made its exploitation through sin impossible. For according to this understanding it was the essence of the law that it be fulfilled not through some action of man but only by faith. Hence, Paul called it in some places " the law of faith " (Rom. 3:27) ; in others, " the law of the Spirit of life " whose " requirement is fulfilled " in those " who walk according to the Spirit " (ch. 8:2 and 4) . Here the law is understood as the eternal will of God which gives life to the dead (ch. 4:17) . If one believed he were able to fulfill God's will in some other way than by " believing " in this " promise " of God himself in his deity, who " gives life to the dead " and " who justifies the ungodly " (v. 5), he would not be giving God the honor due him. He would not be honoring God precisely in the respect in which God wishes to be honored, namely, in the deity by which he calls into being what is not (v. 17) . For it is in this faith that one gives himself to God as one who is nothing before God, receiving his life from him. The mere thought of willing to become righteous before this God through one's own works is an act in which one denies himself to God and sins against him.

In *this* understanding of the law the traditional understanding, in which the law must be fulfilled through action, contains a wholly different meaning. This is so in a twofold way: first, since the law can no longer be religiously worshiped and thus ceases to be the way to salvation; secondly, since the knowledge of the demands of the law becomes the responsibility of man's reason. The admonitions so frequently made in the New Testament to keep oneself free from the " world " have the purpose of reminding one that faith is the decisive thing. As Paul expressed it, that means remembering the distinction between both these forms of the law. For if faith does not cling to this distinction, then it is lost and the old fate comes to power again. This is what Paul meant when he said: " Do not be deceived; God is not mocked, for whatever a man sows, that he will also reap. For he who sows to his own flesh will from the flesh reap corruption; but he who sows to the Spirit will from the Spirit reap eternal life." (Gal. 6:7 f.)

It is the same for responsibility today as it once was for the law with Paul. Through modern subjectivism it has become a fate. This subjectivism, as we have seen (Chapter 10), broke out not least for the reason that soon after the Reformation an understanding of faith had arisen with which faith could not fulfill its proper task. The task was to liberate the law from every kind of religious worship, as Luther helped us to see. Instead, it seemed necessary that the science originating at that time be restricted externally in the name of faith, as it corresponded to the very faith as now conditioned by the law. In defense of its autonomy science appealed to the validity of the reason based on itself, so that reason more and more took the place of faith. The religious teaching of the so-called enthusiasts regarding the " inner light," which was already being propagated during the Reformation, was most effective in encouraging this trend. In the course of things the autonomy of the reason which was established in this way and the responsibility that resulted from it was, as Gerhard

Krüger said, "not simply a matter of a harmless act of meditation on the theory of knowledge. It was, rather, a matter of self-consciousness in the sense of self-assertion against the divine omnipotence" (*op. cit.*, p. 251). In view of the problem of responsibility as we have been dealing with it here, that means that the autonomy of man's reason has been perverted, and with it man's responsibility for the world achieved by deeds. This kind of responsibility was originally made possible by the responsibility that is only to be fulfilled by faith, for it is concerned with the world as God's creation and as an inheritance granted to man as the son of God, and therefore with the wholeness and the health of the world, which it has only in the creatorhood of God. But in the modern time of the autonomy of the reason that whole scheme is changed. Now, when under the influence of subjectivism reason is put in the place of faith, the relation between these two kinds of responsibility is reversed. The responsibility for the wholeness of the world, which the world has only in God's creatorhood, now becomes the aim to be realized by the responsibility that man's action must fulfill.

Thus, what is originally given as God's reality, and what only truly is what it is as it is granted to man by God, is now changed into something that has to be realized by man's works. What is originally granted to man by God is God's deity and creatorhood, enduring in the world as his creation and present to man as son in the world which is his inheritance. Only by faith can man be aware of the nature of what God has originally granted him. Only as man responds by his faith to God's act of giving and in this way is expectant toward it does he participate in the lasting presence of God's deity and creatorhood in the world.

It is obvious that everything here, from man's perspective, depends on faith. Without faith there is nothing but the naked, bare responsibility of man for the world. This responsibility is naked and bare because in it man depends wholly on himself and on what only he can do. Perhaps man has never been so lonely in his world, so dependent upon himself, strange to say, as he is in this responsibility. But whatever modern man may encounter in the world, he encounters himself in everything he meets. He is responsible for himself. That is the unavoidable result of his independence toward the world which imposes this responsibility upon him. In a lecture on " The View of Nature in Modern Physics," Heisenberg has said, " If one attempts on the basis of the situation in modern science to sense the foundation (of our existence) come into motion, one gets the impression that one does not oversimplify if one says that for the first time in the course of history man on this earth finds no other partner or opponent over against him but himself." (In the book *Die Kunst im technischen Zeitalter,* Munich, 1954, p. 52.) And Heidegger did not regard it as a contradiction but as confirmation of Heisenberg's statement when he said in a lecture in the same series, " However, today man nowhere encounters himself, that is, his nature " (*ibid.*, p. 98). We have said the very same thing of responsibility. In it man remains alone with himself. He is without the word by response to which alone can it be true responsibility. Nevertheless, he remains responsible for the world because he must live in it as it has come to be through his action.

We have already said that we are no more able to overcome the fate imposed on us in this responsibility by withdrawing from it than Paul was able to overcome the fate of the law by that means. The responsibility exists by right and not simply for pragmatic reasons. The deeper reason why man must not withdraw from this responsibility is that by doing so he would be giving up his own manhood and the possibility of faith along with it. All we have said about responsibility as it has now developed should not and cannot mean that it is possible to come to faith on the basis of it. For there is a further basis to this responsibility that it cannot recognize by itself. In the form in which the responsibility has now been accepted man is completely chained by that for which he is responsible and by what must be done. Every prospect for something that can really change this situation is blocked. If there were such a thing as liberation from this bondage, that could only be accomplished through something for which the responsibility is responsible. But when that has been achieved, the responsibility is there anew for the results of what is achieved. It cannot be otherwise. If the responsibility remains what it is here, it holds man unavoidably captive to it. Then man is not only imprisoned in the responsibility, but he is also bound in himself by this responsibility. That is the same fact of the matter that the apostle Paul has expressed in such a classic way: " The very commandment which promised life proved to be death to me. For sin, finding opportunity in the commandment, deceived me and by it killed me." (Rom. 7:10 f.)

There is only one possibility of depriving this fate of its power: to go back to the law in the form in which, as Paul said, it is granted for man's life. We have just expressed the authentic reason for this. Responsibility is valid, and man cannot withdraw himself from it or he would give up his own human being and the possibility of faith along with it. Even if that knowledge cannot be achieved out of responsibility itself, the fact persists in it as long as it remains responsibility in some form. For responsibility belongs to what God has granted man in his word. In the responsibility, what God has granted man in his word remains present in its entirety as long as man and the world exist. As we attempted to show earlier, all that is indeed forfeited. But to say it is forfeited does not mean that it no longer exists. It has become fundamentally perverted. Paul could say of the law that although it is directed to man's death, it is still holy, right, and good (v. 12). We must say the same thing about responsibility. Although it has become a fate to us, it could not have become even that had it not been holy, right, and good.

But all this can be said only when faith fulfills the responsibility for the wholeness of man and the world, which only faith can fulfill, and when faith in this responsibility has been aware of God's deity and creatorhood enduring in the world as the original gift to man. Responsibility for the world as man has to achieve it through his action in independent, reasonable decision also belongs to responsibility. For only faith can fulfill the responsibility that encounters the whole world and man. It is the sole justifying faith. But whether it is really understood as the sole justifying faith will be demonstrated when it is seen whether it is capable of safeguarding the independence of man toward the world and the autonomy of its responsibility given with the independence. If this independence and responsibility is safeguarded by faith — and we have seen that only faith can fulfill so proper a task as guarding the freedom of man for God — then man will no longer pervert to the purposes of death what is granted him for life. He will no longer exchange the responsibility as achievable by faith alone for what has to be achieved by his works. The world will then be delivered from the horrible delusion that it would only have a meaning if man gave it one. Thus the force will be removed from the fate of subjectivism.

INDEX